Privilege Through the Looking-Glass

PERSONAL/PUBLIC SCHOLARSHIP

Volume 2

Scope

The *Personal/Public Scholarship* book series values: (1) public scholarship (scholarship that is accessible to academic and popular audiences), and (2) interconnections between the personal and public in all areas of cultural, social, economic and political life. We publish textbooks, monographs and anthologies (original material only).

Please consult www.patricialeavy.com for submission requirements (click the book series tab).

Privilege Through the Looking-Glass

Edited by

Patricia Leavy

SENSE PUBLISHERS
ROTTERDAM/BOSTON/TAIPEI

A C.I.P. record for this book is available from the Library of Congress.

ISBN: 978-94-6351-138-4 (paperback)
ISBN: 978-94-6351-139-1 (hardback)
ISBN: 978-94-6351-140-7 (e-book)

Published by: Sense Publishers,
P.O. Box 21858,
3001 AW Rotterdam,
The Netherlands
https://www.sensepublishers.com/

All chapters in this book have undergone peer review.

Printed on acid-free paper

PRAISE FOR
PRIVILEGE THROUGH THE LOOKING-GLASS

"*Privilege Through the Looking-Glass* offers a varied and profound examination of how privilege functions as the underside of power. This is a powerful and important book about inequality, identity, agency, and the challenge of addressing difference as part of a democratic ethos in a time of growing authoritarianism all over the world. Every educator should read this book."
– Henry A. Giroux, Ph.D., Professor of English and Cultural Studies, McMaster University, and author of *America at War with Itself*

"Patricia Leavy has brought together a group interdisciplinary scholars who have taken up the formidable challenge of analyzing how their own lived experiences are understood and measured by manufactured norms produced historically by systems of mediation (institutional, cultural, social, economic) and intelligibility that are often invisible and that position them differentially (politically) in a structured series of dependent hierarchies that privilege whiteness over non-whiteness, capital over labor, maleness over femaleness, etc. While it is often a privilege to live in the world of theory, we need to remember that when we scratch a theory, we discover biographies, we find histories and we find pain. *Privilege Through the Looking-Glass* is a courageous volume that blends theory, personal experiences, and reflections on contemporary debates over identity. This is a book that is more about the politics of identity than identity politics. It is a powerful testament to the urgency of understanding privilege and deserves to be read widely."
– Peter McLaren, Ph.D., Distinguished Professor in Critical Studies, Chapman University, and author of *Paulo Freire, Che Guevara and the Pedagogy of Revolution*, and *Pedagogy of Insurrection*

"Never was a book that critically interrogates privilege so urgently needed. From microaggressions to macroaggressions, Patricia Leavy's latest book stays true to her commitment to linking the personal and political in public research, and these multiple passionate contributors demand that readers wake up, take action, and do the same in our own work and everyday lives."
– Anne M Harris, Ph.D., Associate Professor, Principal Research Fellow, RMIT University

"*Privilege Through the Looking-Glass* unmasks the casual 'isms' that suppress the best aspects of our humanity, by assembling a powerful and honest collection of parables. Poignant and unflinching, the contributors eschew to the cloak of objectivism to give the hard truth about privilege as a social ill, and the collective responsibility of the conscious community to confront all forms of oppression. Stimulating to the highbrow, yet palatable to the lay, this book has lessons for anyone with the spirit to explore better ways to be themselves and relate to others."
– Ivory A. Toldson, Ph.D., Professor, Counseling Psychology Program, Howard University, and Editor-in-Chief for *The Journal of Negro Education*

"*Privilege Through the Looking-Glass* offers readers a reflective and reflexive response to the confounding and corrosive issues that inform, and sometimes govern, people's everyday lives and identities. In highly accessible and unique ways, this book shines a light on the complexities of cultural life, and in ways that will entice and challenge readers, compelling them to re-think their ways of being with others, and themselves."
– Keith Berry, Ph.D., Associate Professor, Department of Communication, University of South Florida and the National Communication Association Anti-Bullying Task Force Co-Chair

"Marshalling the power of storytelling, *Privilege Through the Looking-Glass* offers a collection of essays wherein experienced scholars confront, challenge, and explicitly discuss everyday forms of racial, sexual, gendered, and ablest privilege embedded in contemporary social life. In so doing, Leavy and the contributors offer an admirable introduction to the many ways the personal is political, and invisible privileges operating at varied levels of society can be made visible and subject to correction. Well-crafted through combinations of scholarly expertise and personal experience, *Privilege Through the Looking-Glass* may be an ideal text for sensitizing students to the myriad of social forces operating within, around, and beyond their own everyday experiences and assumptions."
– J.E. Sumerau, Ph.D., Assistant Professor, Sociology, University of Tampa, and author of *Cigarettes & Wine*

"To be included in Patricia Leavy's world is inspiring but to have the opportunity to read her work on privilege, power, oppression and the expectations or freedoms from persons of diverse backgrounds and statuses, well that's just exhilarating. As a social policy instructor and clinical social worker, I always find opportunities to use Leavy's work with my students, whose testimonies include their own exhilaration in exploring privilege and power and perhaps even discovering their own unexposed privilege."
– **Renita M. Davis, LCSW, PIP, Social Work, Troy University**

Also from Patricia Leavy

Blue

Low-Fat Love
Expanded Anniversary Edition

American Circumstance
Anniversary Edition

Gender & Pop Culture
A Text-Reader
Edited by Adrienne Trier-Bieniek and Patricia Leavy

For more information, visit the author's website
www.patricialeavy.com

To Shalen Lowell,
social justice warrior, treasured friend,
and endless source of support

TABLE OF CONTENTS

ACKNOWLEDGEMENTS

First and foremost, thank you to the contributors. I'm in awe of your bravery and wisdom. Thank you for your hard work and making yourself vulnerable in service of others. Thank you Peter de Liefde, publisher extraordinaire, for your boundless support of social justice projects. Thank you to the entire team at Sense Publishers and Brill, especially Jolanda Karada for your outstanding production coordination. Appreciation to the editorial advisory board members of the *Personal/Public Scholarship* series for your generosity, and to the early reviewers for your generous endorsements. Thank you to Clear Voice Editing for the phenomenal copyediting services.

My deep gratitude to my colleagues, friends, and family, especially Vanessa Alssid, Melissa Anyiwo, Celine Boyle, Pamela DeSantis, Sandra Faulkner, Ally Field, Anne Harris, Libby Hatlan, Laurel Richardson, Monique Robitaille, Jessica Smartt Gullion, and Adrienne Trier-Bieniek. Mr. Barry Mark Shuman, thank you for being my best English teacher and my first sociology teacher. Tori Amos, thank you for illustrating how to build new structures that combine social justice and creativity. To my Facebook community, virtual hugs for the support and comradery. Madeline Leavy-Rosen, I love you. Mark Robins, I love you too. Finally, Shalen Lowell, this one is for you. Thank you for modeling what it means to be a brave, justice warrior in a world too often in need of change. I'm grateful for your friendship in the good times and bad, and endlessly appreciative of all of your support. I could not do any of this work without your clerical, marketing, and research assistance, not to mention all of the times you've helped me rage or laugh, depending on what is needed.

PATRICIA LEAVY

1. INTRODUCTION TO *PRIVILEGE THROUGH THE LOOKING-GLASS*

The true focus of revolutionary change is never merely the oppressive situations which we seek to escape, but that piece of the oppressor which is planted deep within each of us.

(Audre Lorde, 1984, p. 123)

This book seeks to make visible that which is often invisible. It seeks to sensitize us to things we have been taught not to see. Privilege, power, oppression, and domination operate in complex and insidious ways, impacting groups and individuals. And yet, these forces that affect our lives so deeply seem to at once operate in plain sight and lurk in the shadows, making them difficult to discern. There is an expression in sociology that says, "I don't know who discovered water, but I doubt it was a fish". In other words, environments are nearly impossible to perceive when we are immersed in them. This book attempts to expose our environments.

Privilege Through the Looking-Glass is a collection of essays that explore status characteristics in daily life. The essays seek to illustrate that the personal is public. None of us lives in a vacuum. We live in social, historical contexts that shape our experiences. Status characteristics, such as race, class, gender, sexual orientation, religion, education, and ableness have a profound impact on the experiences of groups within society as well as individuals' personal biographies. Through societal institutions (e.g., education, government) as well as the symbolic realm (e.g., images and narratives that circulate via the media), we develop ideas about different groups based on these shared characteristics. This is the essence of socialization, the lifelong process by which we learn the norms and values of our culture as well as how to enact our multiple roles (e.g., student, friend, worker, patriot) in culturally appropriate ways. Through the socialization process we develop taken-for-granted, common sense ideas about the social world and our place within it. These ideas include assumptions and biases that are used to justify social injustice and inequality.

P. Leavy (Ed.), Privilege Through the Looking-Glass, 1–6.
© 2017 Sense Publishers. All rights reserved.

WHAT IS PRIVILEGE?

Privilege refers to the unearned benefits we receive based on our status characteristics. In her groundbreaking essay, Peggy McIntosh (1989) explored White privilege and male privilege. She observed an "invisible knapsack" of unearned benefits or privileges that Whites carry around with them. A few examples of White privilege include speaking to people in positions of power in education or business and knowing you are likely speaking to a person of your own race, going shopping without being followed or harassed, readily finding books and toys for your children that represent characters who look like them, and being pulled over by the police without worrying your race will work against or endanger you. The greatest privilege of all is not recognizing how you benefit from privilege. The inability to see these unearned benefits is a privilege. People who benefit from unearned privileges are generally oblivious to them, as they have been socialized to be. Privilege and power are invisible to those who have it (Kimmel, 2014; McIntosh, 1989). Drawing on McIntosh, Michael Kimmel writes, "To be white, or straight, or male, or middle-class is to be simultaneously ubiquitous and invisible. You're everywhere you look, you're the standard against which everyone else is measured. You're like water, like air" (2014, p. 3). For example, when we talk about race, we think of people of color, not White people, as if they do not embody race. Or consider how we identify males with Mr., which carries no meaning with regard to age or marital status, in contrast with Miss, Ms., and Mrs. for females, which identifies females in relation to their relationship status (Tannen, 2009).

It's difficult to sensitize people to their own privilege in part because of the nature of oppression. Marilyn Frye (2007) explains that oppression is a macroscopic phenomenon and cannot be understood when applying only a microscopic perspective, as we are prone to do in daily life. Frye uses a bird cage analogy to explain how oppression operates. If you focus your eyes on only one wire of a bird cage, you will wonder why the bird doesn't fly freely. One wire alone does not inhibit the bird. You must step back in order to see the *network* of connected wires, which together are as confining as a solid dungeon (Frye, 2007, p. 86). Frye writes this about women's oppression, "...when you look macroscopically you can see it—a network of forces and barriers which are systematically related and which conspire to the immobilization, reduction, and molding of women and the lives we live" (2007, p. 86).

Oppressions are also structurally arranged to operate in concert with each other. For example, sexism and homophobia work together, with each used as a weapon for the other (Pharr, 2007). For instance, consider the use of the word "lesbian" as an insult (a weapon) (Pharr, 2007).

In order to understand how privilege and power operate in complex ways, this book adopts an intersectional approach.

WHAT IS INTERSECTIONALITY?

When it comes to social inequality, people's lives and the organization of power in a given society are better understood as being shaped not by a single axis of social division, be it race or gender or class, but by many axes that work together and influence each other.
(Patricia Hill Collins & Sirma Bilge, 2016, p. 2)

Intersectionality developed in the context of Black feminist activism and thought. During the social justice movements of the 1960s and 1970s, Black feminists expounded many principles of intersectionality in both political contexts and groundbreaking texts, although the term was not yet used (Collins & Bilge, 2016). A major development occurred in 1973 with the formation of the Combahee River Collective (CRC), a collective of Black feminists. Their work has been vital to the elaboration of what became known as intersectionality theory. In their famous 1977 statement, they wrote:

The most general statement of our politics at the present time would be that we are actively committed to struggling against racial, sexual, heterosexual, and class oppression, and see as our particular task the development of integrated analysis and practice based upon the fact that the major systems of oppression are interlocking. The synthesis of these oppressions creates the conditions of our lives. (Combahee River Collective, 1977)

Influenced by this work, Black and Chicana feminists published numerous landmark texts in the 1980s (see the suggested resources at the end of this chapter for examples). Kimberlé Williams Crenshaw (1989, 1991) is credited with coining the term intersectionality to examine how status characteristics *intersect* or overlap.

Identities are not one dimensional or unitary. One simultaneously inhabits a body that carries race, gender, and class (as well as sexual orientation and ableness). I am not simply a woman. I am a White, middle-upper class, able-bodied woman. The interconnections of these identities shape my positioning in the social order, and thus my identity and experiences with privilege and oppression. My experiences will differ greatly from those of a woman with different racial and economic statuses, for example. Under intersectionality theory, race, class, and gender (and other social identities) are viewed as "interlocking systems of oppression" that shape domination and subordination (Collins, 1990, 2007). Further, there are three dimensions of oppression: institutional, symbolic, and individual. The latter refers to how our own biographies are shaped by race, class, gender, sexual orientation, and ableness. It is here that the mission of this book takes shape. How are our individual biographies differently shaped by status characteristics and the structures of inequality they produce? By exploring personal stories, the authors in this volume also shine a light on the institutional and symbolic dimensions of oppression.

WHY STORIES?

Personal stories are uniquely powerful. Stories connect us to one another. They reveal people and their circumstances, inviting others to develop new understandings, awareness, and at times, empathy. Whether our experiences are similar or different, authentic stories resonate. We are each an authority on our own story. When I developed the idea for this project, I knew it would center on personal stories.

This book is called *Privilege Through the Looking-Glass*. A looking-glass is a mirror; it reflects back at us. Thanks to Lewis Carroll, a looking-glass also implies that what is seen is different from what is expected. The contributors have been asked to look deeply into a mirror, excavating their experiences and confronting how privilege operates in ways that might be different from what others see on the surface. The looking-glass metaphor ultimately reflects how the essays in this book turn privilege inside out, exposing that which is otherwise concealed.

This book is not about personal stories for the sake of personal sharing. I sought out well-respected interdisciplinary scholars and writers to share their stories as a means of *connecting the personal and the public*. The contributors in this volume could all easily write traditional scholarly pieces about privilege. Instead, I asked them to write personal essays about status characteristics in their own lives, in any form or manner they saw fit. That was a big ask. They would have to be quite courageous. They were. Instead of relying solely on academic scholarship, these authors agreed to delve deeply into their own lives, exposing personal experiences, thoughts, feelings, and vulnerabilities. Understanding the goal of this volume, they have either made explicit connections to the institutional and cultural dimensions of privilege and oppression in their essays, through interweaving the personal and public, or via the discussion questions or activities at the end of their chapter. As you will see, there are also threads across the readings. For example, self-acceptance is a theme in many of the essays. I applaud the contributors for bravely and boldly sharing their personal experiences and for situating them within larger cultural processes in order to invite you to engage in meaningful self and social reflection.

SUGGESTED RESOURCES

Anzaldúa, G. (1987). *Borderlands/La Frontera*. San Francisco, CA: Aunt Lute Books.
Collins, P. H., & Bilge, S. (2016). *Intersectionality*. Cambridge, UK: Polity Press.
Combahee River Collective Statement. (1977). http://circuitous.org/scraps/combahee.html
Combahee River Collective website http://combaheerivercollective.weebly.com/
Lorde, A. (1984). *Sister outsider*. Trumansberg, NY: The Crossing Press.

REFERENCES

Collins, P. H. (1990). Black feminist thought in the matrix of domination. In P. H. Collins (Ed.), *Black feminist thought: Knowledge, consciousness, and the politics of empowerment* (pp. 221–238). London: HarperCollins.
Collins, P. H. (2007). Toward a new vision: Race, class, and gender as categories of analysis and connection. In S. M. Shaw & J. Lee (Eds.), *Women's voices, feminist visions: Classic and contemporary readings* (pp. 76–84). Oregon, OR: Oregon State University.
Collins, P. H., & Bilge, S. (2016). *Intersectionality*. Cambridge, UK: Polity Press.
Combahee River Collective Statement (1977). http://circuitous.org/scraps/combahee.html
Crenshaw, K. W. (1989). Demarginalizing the intersection of race and sex: A black feminist critique of antidiscrimination doctrine, feminist theory and antiracist politics. *University of Chicago Legal Forum, 140*, 139–167.
Crenshaw, K. W. (1991). Mapping the margins: Intersectionality, identity politics, and violence against women of color. *Stanford Law Review, 43*, 1249–1299.
Frye, M. (2007). Oppression. In S. M. Shaw & J. Lee (Eds.), *Women's voices, feminist visions: Classic and contemporary readings* (pp. 84–86). Oregon, OR: Oregon State University.
Kimmel, M. S. (2014). Introduction: Toward a sociology of the superordinate. In M. S. Kimmel & A. L. Ferber (Eds.), *Privilege: A reader* (3rd ed., pp. 1–12). Boulder, CO: Westview Press.
Lorde, A. (1984). *Sister outsider*. Trumansberg, NY: The Crossing Press.
McIntosh, P. (1989, July/August). White privilege: Unpacking the invisible knapsack. *Peace and Freedom Magazine*, 10–12. Women's International League for Peace and Freedom, Philadelphia, PA.

Pharr, S. (2007). Homophobia: A weapon of sexism. In S. M. Shaw & J. Lee (Eds.), *Women's voices, feminist visions: Classic and contemporary readings* (pp. 87–91). Oregon, OR: Oregon State University.

Tannen, D. (2009). There is no unmarked woman. In S. Maasik & J. Solomon (Eds.), *Signs of life in the U.S.A.: Readings on popular culture for writers* (6th ed., pp. 620–625). Boston, MA: Bedford/St. Martin's.

ROBIN M. BOYLORN

2. UNPACKING (UN)PRIVILEGE OR FLESH TONES, RED BONES, AND SEPIA SHADES OF BROWN

PRIVILEGE/D POSITIONS

In Peggy McIntosh's seminal essay, *White Privilege: Unpacking the Invisible Knapsack*, she reckons with the revelation that as a white person she enjoys race privileges to which she, and most other white people, are oblivious. Her lack of awareness of her own privilege exposes the limitations of our personal politics and reinforces the importance of understanding the nuances of identity and privilege. For example, white people will always benefit from white privilege in a white supremacist, capitalist culture. Men will always receive unearned advantages in a patriarchal system designed for their success. Heterosexual people will always be privileged in a heteronormative and trans, bi and homophobic society that is hierarchically designed to render nonheterosexuality invisible and/or abnormal. Able-bodied people will continue to be recognized to the exclusion of others in a system that is both ableist and ageist. By definition, social and cultural privileges are invisible and institutional. We are not socialized to be cognizant of our privileges. Flat-out denial and defiant resistance are the frequent responses of privileged folk when called out about their inherited and unfair advantages. Many times, we exhibit willful ignorance about our personal invisible knapsacks of privilege, while being hyper-aware of the ways other people fail to acknowledge and account for their own. When highlighted, privilege is the hot potato nobody wants to be caught holding in their hand.

Acknowledging privilege jeopardizes our worldview and self-concept. People with privilege generally go their whole lives without ever being forced to reckon with the ways their everyday experiences of normalcy are actually exceptional. If you are a white woman, it is often an afterthought to consider how your race privilege distinguishes you from women of color, thereby offering you opportunities, benefits, and open doors that would be impossible or difficult for black women to walk through. If you are a cisgendered, heterosexual woman of color, you may not recognize that while you experience discrimination due to your race, you also experience privilege

P. Leavy (Ed.), Privilege Through the Looking-Glass, 7–12.
© *2017 Sense Publishers. All rights reserved.*

because your gender performance matches the biological sex you were assigned at birth and you are sexually and romantically interested in men. While privilege is often attached to the mythical "normal" representation of a white, heterosexual, educated, financially secure, able-bodied male, we all enjoy some social privileges. As a black woman, I face the double jeopardy of race and sex oppression, but I also enjoy privileges associated with my educational attainment, social class, ability, and sexual orientation.

Identity politics are complicated. It is possible to be simultaneously privileged and marginalized. It is possible to be progressive in one area and shortsighted in another. It is possible to "get it" when it comes to the ways you experience discrimination, and not "get it" when discrimination happens tangentially. The power of privilege can contaminate good intentions. Allies are not immune to it. "Good people" can't wash it off. Multiple and generational oppressions don't remove it. It usually exists ubiquitously and without notice, except for those who don't have it.

Privilege is not something to be ashamed of, however. Social and cultural benefits are structural, so we couldn't opt out of our positions of privilege even if we wanted to. I could never wake up one day and decide that I'm tired of the ways my heterosexual identity oppresses those who identify as non-heterosexual. I can't exchange it for something else. While we can't trade in our social identities or put our ethnicities on layaway, we can be informed about privilege and be proactive about using our privilege to help those who don't have it. More importantly, we can help others understand how privilege works, and use the platform and legitimacy that comes with our particular privileges to support others. But the first and hardest step is acknowledging that you have privilege(s) in the first place.

COLORISM, COLORBLINDNESS, & COLORING BOOKS

People of color, regardless of their other social identity markers, have a peculiar relationship with privilege because of the un-privilege of being un-white (Boylorn, 2006, 2011a, 2011b). Race, or skin color, is a visible marker of identity that is associated with histories and legacies of subordination, discrimination, and disenfranchisement. Despite claims to the contrary, the twenty-first century did not represent a shift in racism (there is no such thing as reverse racism), a black president did not guarantee us post-racialism (there is no such thing as post-racialism), and the existence of Rachel Dolezal does not suddenly make blackness an interchangeable option for curious white folk who want to see what it's like to be black (there is no such thing as transracialism). Whiteness is a privilege only afforded to those who are either born white or who can pass for white. Historically, dark-skinned people of color are always and automatically excluded from whiteness (Blay, 2014).

***

In 1985, there were only primary and secondary colors in the eight-count Crayola crayon box, and similar but less splendid versions in the generic brand my mama bought me, alongside a coloring book, as a consolation gift on my sister's ninth birthday. Even though my sister and I were born two years, five months, and two days apart, my mother would give each of us a small present to open when we were celebrating the others' birthday. These gestures were necessary with daughters who were so decidedly different in appearance and demeanor. It was especially important in 1985, the year I learned (from my peers at school) that being dark-skinned with a light-skinned sister meant I was less pretty, less smart, less valued, and therefore less loved.

Before starting school, I was jealous of my sister for all the regular reasons. She was older, so she experienced all the firsts first. I shrank in the shadow of her accomplishments, her intelligence, her light skin. Though I didn't have the language at the time, I picked up on the ways she was favored by adults and strangers. They would gush over the built-in beauty of her skin and curly hair. Even school peers regularly recounted my sister's inherent goodness, insisting we didn't have the same daddy because she was "light, bright, and damn near white." I was just black. The contrast was stark and the weight of dark-skinnedness felt like forever.

***

Colorblindness is the well-intentioned mantra of progressive and liberal white folk who want to announce that they are not racist. "I don't see color," they claim, when talking about racial politics. "I just see people".

When this happens in my classroom, I announce that while I appreciate the gesture, claiming to not see color is not only ingenuine, it is offensive.

"Of course you see color," I say, holding out my arm in demonstration. "I am a black woman—my race is not something you can NOT see".

"Not me, Dr. B!"

"Race doesn't matter to me".

Discomfort and guilt fill the room as I explain, "Being a black woman colors and shapes my entire existence. To not see my color diminishes me, disappears me. And it is dishonest because my blackness is really all you see, the first thing you see when you look at me. To tell me you don't see my blackness means you don't see me".

9

I understand what my white students mean, but I insist on talking it out. "Colorblindness is not a cure, I promise you," I say, challenging how they have been socialized to think about race. "We can't go around pretending everybody is white. I'm not white and that matters."

"My parents taught me not to 'see color'".

"Seeing race is not racist," I say.

***

While colorblindness is a well-intentioned effort to deny the existence of race and therefore the possibility of racial preference, it denies the inevitability of racial difference and the existence and impact of white racism. Colorblindness also ignores the fact that people of color are people of color, and that their worth is not and should not be attached to their likeness to whiteness (color or culture). Colorblindness can also lead to colorism denial.

While blackness prevents folk of color from ever experiencing white privilege, there are skin color privileges that exist within the black community, known as colorism. By definition, colorism is skin color stratification that privileges light-skinned people and disadvantages darker-skinned people. This color(ism) hierarchy, not unlike white supremacy, attaches value and beauty to light complexion (Blay, 2010). Darker-skinned people experience prejudice and discrimination, which leads to internalized racism and oftentimes resentment.

The narratives that are most public are the experiences of women of color. For example, in the dual documentaries, *Dark Girls* and *Light Girls*, directed by D. Channsin Berry and Bill Duke (both black men), black women discuss their anxieties and experiences of trauma as "dark" or "light" skinned women of color. Instead of providing a much-needed opportunity for discussion, the narratives became combative and competitive, largely focused on beauty politics and desirability to men. In addition to ignoring the intersectionality of these women's experiences and the myriad of issues that contribute to our colorist culture, the narratives revealed pain and pointed fingers. Discussions about colorism need to be more broad, more inclusive, and focus less on the extremes (of very light or very dark) and more on representation of the in-betweenness of skin hues, which is representative of many black women who are left out of the conversation and who, themselves, feel "not (light or dark) enough".

Dr. Yaba Blay, author of *One Drop: Shifting the Lens on Race*, prefers the term, "skin color politics" over "color complex, colorism, or color struck" because it references the larger and systemic issues that are in play when we are discussing how colorism works within the black community. Blay (2010) states, "Skin color is a very much political construct...there continues to be a certain amount of privilege, both actual and assumed, associated with the tone of one's skin color" (p. 30). These politics can be attributed to the social advantages afforded to light-skinned people of color (because they can pass for white), and to the low self-esteem or feelings of worthlessness that some dark-skinned people of color experience as a result of being teased and demonized because of their skin color (and the lack of mainstream representation).

Robust discussions of colorism or "skin color politics" (Blay, 2016) among people of color are just as important as discussions of racism among white people. An acknowledgment of privilege is not a denial of oppression. We can and often do occupy both spaces at once, so there needs to be space and opportunity for black folk to deconstruct colorism to better understand and articulate what "color" means within the black community, and why. While it is important for white folk to understand white privilege, it is equally important for folk of color to acknowledge and understand the implications of white privilege on blackness, and how it manifests in colorism.

VIEWING RECOMMENDATIONS

1. *Dark Girls* documentary
2. *Light Girls* documentary

ACTIVITIES

1. Get a popular magazine and compare images of white women and women of color. What are the implied and implicit messages about what beauty is and who attains it? In other words, what are consistent qualities found in white women in the ads? What are consistent physical qualities found in women of color?
2. Make a list of adjectives or descriptions associated with white and black, light and dark. Discuss the difference between how we are conditioned and socialized to think about blackness/darkness and whiteness/lightness, and how that translates into feelings and perceptions of race and color.
3. Compile a list of at least 10 descriptions for skin colors/tones. With a peer, describe each complexion without naming race. Then, discuss the racial implications of language and how we race and/or (e)rase identity with words.
4. After watching *Dark Girls* and *Light Girls* (full films or excerpts from each) as a class, compare and discuss the narratives offered in each. Identify the

similarities and differences in the shared experiences and create a holistic list of traumas each group experiences, linked to their color. Then, draft (and time permitting, perform) short skits to demonstrate how women of color might begin dialogue with each other, across those differences. Use, when possible, specific language and testimonies from the film in the script.

DISCUSSION QUESTIONS

1. What might be a better term, other than colorblindness, to represent a commitment to racial equality?
2. What are some privileges and consequences of skin complexion? Consider the difference in this question for white folk versus folk of color.
3. In what ways does colorism, alongside racism, dictate what is constituted as beautiful?
4. What color/shade would you describe yourself and why? Do you believe that others would agree? In what ways has your color translated to how you are treated by others?
5. Do you think light-skinned privilege exists? In what ways?
6. How and why are "skin color politics" gendered?
7. What are some negative names, labels, or slang terms associated with blackness or dark skin that reinforces colorism?
8. What role might colorism play as we move into a progressively biracial and multicultural society?

REFERENCES

Blay, Y. A. (2010). Pretty color n good hair: Creole women in New Orleans and the politics of identity. In R. E. Spillers & K. R. Moffitt (Eds.), *Blackberries and redbones: Critical articulations of black hair/body politics in Africana communities* (pp. 29–52). Cresskill, NJ: Hampton Press.

Blay, Y. A. (2014). *One drop: Shifting the lens on race*. Philadelphia, PA: BlackPrint.

Boylorn, R. M. (2006). E pluribus unum: Out of many, one. *Qualitative Inquiry, 12*(4), 651–680.

Boylorn, R. M. (2011a). Gray or for colored girls who are tired of chasing rainbows: Race and reflexivity. *Cultural Studies ↔ Critical Methodologies, 11*(2), 178–186.

Boylorn, R. M. (2011b). Black kids' (B.K.) stories: Ta(l)king (about) race outside of the classroom. *Cultural Studies ↔ Critical Methodologies, 11*(1), 59–70.

McIntosh, P. (1997). White privilege: Unpacking the invisible knapsack. In B. Schneider (Ed.), *Race: An anthology in the first person* (pp. 120–126). New York, NY: Three Rivers Press.

ADRIENNE TRIER-BIENIEK

3. MEN HUG ME AT WORK

Juxtaposing Privilege with Everyday Sexism

As a feminist who studies inequality and a sociologist who teaches classes focused on privilege, my grasp of the many ways I am privileged is probably more heightened than the average person. I am aware, for example, that when I want a drink of water I can turn on the tap to receive clean, cold water. When I am hungry, I need only to head to my refrigerator or pantry. I have the ability to order food from a take-out place when I don't feel like cooking. When I am cold, I turn on the heat. I drive to work and don't have to worry about the cost of gas or the amount of money I spend on tolls during my commute. One summer day, after I had completed a 5k run for charity, the alternator in my car blew, causing me to lose control of the steering. After I pulled over (and stopped freaking out), I called my husband, whose status as a supervisor at his hospital allowed him to leave without any infraction. He came and got me in our second car and called AAA, a service for which we pay $85 per year. They towed my car to the dealership, who fixed it in a day's time. This happened in June, and because my school offers extra pay for professors who teach in the summer, I could afford the $1700 bill that came with the new alternator, new water pump, and new rear brakes. On a macro level, I am perceived as white and female in my daily life. (Both are true, although there is a lot of Native American on my father's side. On my grandmother's death certificate, her race was listed as "Indian" along with an ethnicity of German and Irish.) I am heterosexual, married, and educated.

Most of my life has been spent existing in this awareness of my own privilege while also trying to combat experiences with oppression. I was painfully aware of inequality as a child. I grew up in the countryside of northwestern Michigan, an area where farming communities lined the edge of Lake Michigan and tractor crossing signs were as common as one-stoplight towns. In my county, there were more dirt roads than paved, impassable after rain and snow. My town was small, a population of a little more than 1,400, and mainly white. My high school had roughly 300 students in attendance but

P. Leavy (Ed.), *Privilege Through the Looking-Glass, 13–20.*
© 2017 Sense Publishers. All rights reserved.

only two were African American. We did have a handful of migrant workers, mainly Mexican kids whose families moved back and forth between my town and cities in Texas, Arizona, and New Mexico. One would think this would add some sense of diversity to my school, but the families rarely stayed in town past September, only to return again in mid-May to long, hard days harvesting in our farming community for low pay.

My parents were situated firmly in the middle-class section of the tax bracket. As social workers, my dad worked with abused children and my mom was stationed in a nursing home. They had enough money to keep us afloat. I attended weekly dance classes, and every summer we took a family vacation. If they struggled, I didn't know about it. Christmas was met with lots of gifts, dolls, sleds, and once, after a solid six months of campaigning, a new Nintendo. (That's the original Nintendo, for those of you who are wondering which system I am referencing.) We lived in an old farmhouse, built in 1913, which sat on 10 acres. My parents spent much of their free time and money renovating the house and gardens.

As I grew up and started working, first in odd jobs which turned into summer jobs, and then in my first career as an activist and second career as an academic, my experiences with privilege became juxtaposed with the everyday sexism I encountered. I would learn that, even though I am quite privileged, I am also a woman in a society that is based in patriarchal structures. Being privileged is not an automatic force field that wards off oppression, just as oppression does not mean that one cannot still hold a certain amount of privilege.

As I began building my career, I encountered enough unwanted touching, grabbing, mansplaining, harassment, old-fashioned ogling, and blatant misogyny to conclude that when you are a woman at work, men are going to try and hug you. Here are some examples of the institutional and everyday sexism that I have encountered, followed by some encounters friends have allowed me to share.

My first job was at a gift shop; I was 16 and hired as a sales clerk. I would watch as kids put their grimy hands on display cases I had just cleaned, and I found more than one dirty diaper shoved in corners of the store. I folded and refolded brightly colored shirts with the town logo splashed across the front. I became used to customers telling me that I had ruined Christmas because the shop didn't carry a certain Beanie Baby. I worked eight to ten hours a day with no break, and my feet swelled so much that they grew half a size in one summer.

It was also at this shop that I began to notice male privilege. Men would come in after a round of golf or a day of boating and drinking and browse as they waited for their wives to finish lunch at the restaurant next door. They found entertainment in pressuring me to try on clothes so they could see what it would look like on their wives. I always declined. They would only chuckle and plead, "Just put it on and let us see what it looks like!" Once, a man asked me what size my gift-shop-issue top was, and when I said, "I don't know, a large?" he grabbed the tag in the back, read it, and announced with glee that it was an extra-large.

When I later took a job as a cashier at a local restaurant, a man saw me reading the newspaper. It was 2000, an election year, and George W. Bush was vying for the presidency with Al Gore. "Who are you voting for?" he asked.

"I haven't decided," I lied.

"Decide!" he shouted in my face. "Vote Bush!" He threw his money on the counter. These are not encounters my male friends have experienced.

I first experienced workplace harassment at age 18, when I was working as an assistant director at our local community theater. I liked this work. I got to be creative by having some say in casting decisions, and was tasked with digging through antique shops for items that could be used as props. We were producing a musical called *The Christmas Schooner* and, not content with the local talent, the director hired an equity actor (read: paid actor) to play the main character of Peter Stossel. Equity Actor Mike Piper (not his real name) was hired (because he knew the playwright) and joined the cast late in the rehearsals. He was in his late thirties, he towered over me (I am five feet three inches tall, he was somewhere around six foot four), was pale with dark brown hair and brown eyes, and had broad shoulders and a head the shape of a pumpkin. The day he arrived, I greeted him in front of the theater and introduced myself. "Nice to meet you," he said. "Let me show you something. This is your most important job." He walked me through the dark theater to the back stage and over to a large black shelf next to the props cage. He pointed at the coffee pot and said, "Your most important job is to make sure this is full all of the time." He smiled, literally patted me on top of my curly blonde head, and walked away. A few days later I was standing at the prop table when he came in through the loading dock door. The light was so bright in the windowless room that I was temporarily blinded. He approached the table and gathered me into a huge hug. "Thanks," he sighed after letting me go. "I really needed that."

Note: I did not know Equity Actor Mike Piper. We had been in contact for less than a week, but he had clearly decided it was fine to grab me and press his body against mine for extended periods of time whenever he thought he needed it. He made the decision to use my body as his own form of comfort. At work. In a professional setting where he was being paid. I spent the next month dodging his hugs and the frequent grabbing of my shoulders, head, and arms. Any way you slice it, it is weird and gross for a man in his late 30s to repeatedly touch and grab an 18-year-old girl at work.

At 20, I filed my first sexual harassment claim. I had a summer job at a local state park that I loved; I got to be outside all day long and was left alone for extended periods of time. Yes, the work could be disgusting – people treat bathrooms and shower rooms differently when they are not at home. The work was also hard. I drove tractors, inserted snow blinds in the fall, cut down trees with chainsaws, dug holes for posts, and scraped dead fish off the beach. I had to face more than one angry camper who had been fined or asked to leave after staying past their reservation date, smoking weed in the woods, parking illegally, having loud sex in their tent, or bringing glass bottles to the beach. Still, for an introvert who can happily exist for days without human interaction, having a job where I was independent and allowed to read after I completed my work was wonderful.

My first day on the job, I encountered Aaron (also not his real name). He was nice enough and spent some time giving me a tour of the ranger station. Once I knew my way around, I was sent to clean the windows. I was bent over a cabinet, sweating and scrubbing, when Aaron walked in to drop off supplies. Later that day, another ranger, whom we will call Trent, mentioned that Aaron wanted to know if I had a boyfriend. "He likes your butt and was talking about how big and juicy it is in those pants. He said he wants to squeeze it like a peach."

I didn't know what to say. All I could manage was, "Ok. Thanks for telling me?" In the coming days, I frequently noticed Aaron staring at my body, and Trent shared many sexual comments that Aaron had made about me.

Later that summer, someone found a blue tank top left behind by a child. Aaron brought to it me and said, "You should try this on for me and model it. You'd look good in it." I sighed and insisted that it wouldn't fit. "Exactly," he said with a smile. That smile was the last straw. I was done with his behavior. I marched into my boss' office, slammed the tank top down on his desk, and recanted all the conversations I had overheard, witnessed, or participated in with Aaron. I conjured up all my conviction and said, "This is sexual harassment." He calmly agreed. An investigation took place and Aaron was transferred to another park. He wasn't punished. He was transferred with the same pay, seniority, and position. As sympathetic as my boss was, there was no consideration that Aaron would repeat this behavior with someone else.

During my first year as a graduate assistant, I was asked out by a student. I was given funding to be an assistant to a professor who was teaching a criminology course. The student had spent the semester trying to flirt with me (and ignoring my wedding ring). I thought it was strange and uncomfortable that this student was pursuing me, and since I was in charge of grading his major project, I didn't want to be perceived as showing any favoritism. When I told my supervising professor that I didn't like the attention, she replied, "Why? This should make you feel good. Like you've still 'got it'".

Later that semester, another graduate student took some of the writing I had posted in the class online forum and turned it in as his own work. When I told my professor, she encouraged me to "blow it off." These examples demonstrate that institutionalized sexism isn't just about the ways men oppress women. Rather, both women and men are capable of sustaining sexist practices. It is the attitude that is sexist, not the gender of the offender.

One would think that I would be shielded from workplace oppression in the world of academia. One would be wrong. In the decade I have spent as a professor, I have amassed enough experiences of oppression or harassment to fill a used car lot. Students have attempted to intimidate me into giving them a better grade by harassing me, generally online or via email. Many male students have come to my office and insisted that we talk with the door closed. This act, while probably innocent, makes me nervous as I have had enough students attempt to badger or hit on me in order to get the grade they want. One student decided that he would flirt his way to a passing grade and would greet me with a "Heeeeyyyyy Professor," followed by a wink. Once, after we had a conversation during office hours about his planning skills, I brought him a planner that is handed out for free in Student Services. His response was, "Do you know what this means? It means you were thinking about me last night." As he spoke, his words got breathy and he put his head close to mine while lightly touching my shoulder. I have had to turn students over to chairs and deans because their emails were so hostile and threatening that I felt unsafe conversing with them. I have never had to call security on a student but, as a department chair, I have had to walk other female faculty through how to make that call.

Yet, I recognize that I still hold power in the student-professor dynamic. I have a certain amount of privilege when these offenses occur. However, the institutional sexism I have experienced from colleagues has disheartened me the most. I once encountered an older male colleague chatting with another man in our department's mailroom. The men stared at my body and commented on it in another language, assuming that I didn't understand them. I grabbed the large box I had come in for, turned around, and asked if they were going to keep staring at me or open the door so I could leave.

In meetings, I am repeatedly asked to take notes, make coffee, and provide colleagues who missed the meeting with the minutes. The men on these committees have never been tasked with these "secretarial" duties. I have been told to "smile" and "relax" when debates about departmental issues are held. Male supervisors often imply that women are catty and have even suggested that conflict among women can be resolved by "hugging it out." A woman on the hiring committee for my position noted that she wanted to hire a man in my place and, on my first day, asked me when I planned on taking leave to have children. I have been followed by campus security into my classroom and asked, "Where is the professor" or told "You can't be in here without the professor".

I was once a member of a committee tasked with reviewing data for the University's re-accreditation proceedings. We floated ideas via email before meeting. Privately, a man on the committee told me that my ideas were in sync with his own, but on the email thread, he discredited my plans when he realized another man (in a position higher than ours) disagreed. Then, at the first meeting, both men took my ideas and presented them to the group as their own. Everyone acted as if the idea was new and applauded their creativity.

Perhaps the most dangerous part of institutional sexism is that it is easily ignored or written off as an individual problem. Yet, even if we take a micro-level stance, a little bit of investigation would reveal similar stories of gender-based, sexist practices. When I asked some friends to share their stories of everyday sexism in the workplace, I received several examples which fall in line with the themes of my own experiences. One friend talked about the poor air quality at her job. She and her (female) colleagues came down with serious respiratory infections and complained to their supervisor, but it wasn't until a man moved into their office space that the problem was fixed. When she asked why it took hiring this new person to get the issue resolved, she was told, "All ladies are constantly complaining about the thermostat. We assumed that was the issue until Mr. X moved in and told us how bad it was".

Another friend, an attorney, is sometimes asked if she is the paralegal, receptionist, or court reporter when she arrives in court. (Nothing is degrading about any of these positions, but the assumption that women in court cannot be attorneys is everyday sexism.) She is usually met with skepticism or disbelief when she states that she is the attorney for the respondent.

A cousin of mine works as at a bar and deals with sexism on a routine basis. A table of men once spent $90 on beer and left only a $3 tip after she wouldn't give them her phone number. When she mentioned this to her boss, he suggested that she should just give out her number, and then joked to another customer, "I'm such a cool guy, I already have it".

One night, while working in an art gallery, a friend was asked by a stranger if he could just sit and watch her work because she was "pretty hot." When she told him that his request was creepy, he tried to beg money from her and became irate when she wouldn't give him any. He said "This is bullshit! Who is in charge here?" He refused to believe that she was in charge. He got in her face and said, "No! I mean the man! I need to talk to the man!" She kept a box cutter in her pocket after that encounter.

These stories illustrate the benign nature of institutional sexism. Perhaps you read these and argued against their actual impact, something that would be connected to sexism becoming engrained in our society. The danger of institutional sexism is that it allows us to judge and become complacent with someone else's experiences. Rather than allowing people who feel oppressed to own their stories, there is a need to discount them. The ability to shut down their stories and experiences lies in how much privilege we hold. Maybe when you read these examples, you decided that they weren't that big of a deal, or that the women in these situations should just leave their job. Or perhaps you have had similar experiences, and felt that this behavior didn't bother you, so why should it bother anyone else? This is the result of the juxtaposition of privilege and institutional sexism. Oppression comes in all sorts of packages. Being able to analyze it is key, particularly when it comes to everyday behaviors that enforce sexism.

DISCUSSION QUESTIONS

1. If the author didn't like her job, particularly if it was only summer work, why didn't she quit and find another job? How is this further complicated when we are discussing long-term employment or careers?

2. In what ways do you feel you have privilege? Think about your gender, race, social class, religion, ability/disability, sexual orientation, age, etc.
3. Have you ever experienced institutional sexism while at work? What did you do about it?
4. Is everyday sexism something that can be solved? What steps would need to be taken?

CHRISTOPHER N. POULOS

4. THE VOICE OF WHITE MALE POWER AND PRIVILEGE

An Autoethnography

BARRIERS AND OPENINGS

I grew up in the segregated deep South, mostly in the suburbs of Atlanta, during the 1960s. At the time, I did not know we were segregated, parsed into discrete categories of black and white. Sure, I knew black people existed – we even had an African-American housekeeper, though nobody called them African Americans back then. In fact, all around Georgia and the deep South, the preferred terminology was "nigger," the somewhat politer "negro," or the slightly ambiguous "colored." I don't think I ever really noticed that we did not live in the same neighborhoods. I just knew that everyone in my neighborhood – and, for that matter, in my school and church – was white. But I never really thought of us as "white." I just thought of us as, well, normal. After all, we were who we saw on TV, at church, and in school. It never occurred to me to think that there were other kinds of "normal," in other places, with different kinds of people.

I remember when it started to dawn on me that maybe differences between black and white were bigger for some people than for others. In the summer of 1967, as I stood on the cusp of turning 10, my mom took us to see the newly released Disney film, *The Jungle Book*, at the famous Fox Theatre in downtown Atlanta. As we walked along the street toward the box office, I noticed a little door that said, "Colored Entrance".

"Mom, what's that door for?"

"It's for the negroes, honey."

"Why?"

"Well…just because."

"Oh."

We bought our tickets, and I noticed that there were stairs labeled "Balcony."

"Mom! Can we sit in the balcony?"

P. Leavy (Ed.), *Privilege Through the Looking-Glass, 21–26.*

"No, honey."

"Why not?"

"Because that's for the colored people."

"So? Can we sit there too?"

She paused for a moment, then grinned and said, "Well, why not?"

And so, we broke the color barrier, three white folk sitting in the front row of the balcony, watching a movie about friendship and co-mingling and sacrifice in the jungle, with a packed balcony of very polite "colored folk." Of course, all this Jim Crow stuff was supposed to end years earlier, but change was slow in coming. Looking back on this incident today, I feel certain that at least some of them didn't want us there, but what were they going to do about it? I doubt I noticed, but my mom was likely aware of their deferential, if feigned, politeness. Of course, they were not free to go downstairs.

On September 8, 1970, my first day of seventh grade at Clifton Elementary School, I found myself arriving later than I liked. I wanted to scope out a good seat by the window, toward the back, but by the time I arrived, I was stuck with two choices: third seat from front on the row by the door, or the front seat right by the teacher's desk. I knew better than *that*, so I chose the former. As I retrieved my notebook from my book bag, I heard an odd sound, kind of like air escaping a tire. I turned to see this kid – whose name, I later learned, was Ralph Jones – standing at the door, grinning widely. Ralph was as black as anyone I'd ever seen, and he had the biggest, whitest, most disarming smile imaginable. He was also the first (and, for this year at least, the only) black kid to ever set foot in this school. Everyone stared at him. He checked out the room, grinning, and strode confidently to the only remaining empty desk, right next to Mrs. Eaton's desk, too close for comfort. He seemed unfazed.

After 16 years of resistance against Brown v. Board of Education, Georgia had finally been forced to desegregate the schools. Ralph was the first to break the color barrier at good old Clifton. He was also the smartest kid I had ever met, and used his sharp wit to both disarm and wither anyone who tried to push him around. The school was full of the children of rednecks, so he was tested daily. He passed the test by being smarter, bigger, stronger, faster, and wittier than any of them. I quickly decided to befriend him.

Since we were both smart and athletic, we stuck together and used our talents to our advantage. Although Ralph was better than me at most everything, I realized that I had an edge. The teachers favored me. Adults in general favored me. When we went places together, the adults didn't address him; they talked to me. One day, I took him home with me to play, to check out the woods behind my house, and to hang out in my treehouse. We walked into the living room and found my great grandmother sitting on the couch talking with my mom. *"Damn. I wish I'd known she'd be here,"* I thought.

Before I could formulate a plan, she turned to my mom and said, "Who's the nigger?"

Just what I was afraid of. Ralph and I looked at each other. With a grin, he answered, "I don't see one, do you?"

"Nope," I reply. "You must be mistaken, Grandma!" We ran through the kitchen and tumbled into the backyard, laughing.

This was the dawning of my racial consciousness. As I attended the first integrated high school in the area, where race riots erupted in the fall of 1971 and again in the spring of 1972, I gradually realized – as I saw it in stark relief and bloody fights – that some people in this world are full of hate and have a damn hard time letting go of their prejudices. Some are willing to bleed just to hold on. I also realized that our society automatically favors me, blond haired, blue eyed, pale skinned me. The white kid from a middle-class family. It was almost surreal how easy it all was for me. School was designed for me, the smart kid who liked to read and write for fun, who did what's expected of him, and who was fluent in the ways of the culture that created the institution. I always executed my assignments flawlessly and on time. It didn't hurt that my mom was a school teacher. She taught us the ropes at home. The rules of this game were almost second nature. I didn't know that there was any other way to approach school than seeking and achieving success. Like I said, I had some advantages. I was favored. *Privileged.*

Holding a position at or near the top of the class can have some disadvantages. Sometimes, the kids at the other end of the spectrum resent you. Still, the advantages definitely outweighed the downsides. After all, the system rewards the kid with straight A's, and the other kids figured out that if they hung out with me, they might learn something or gain some advantage by association. So, mostly, I was in a good position socially. Like I said, favored. Privileged. I fit. It was all too easy for me. While Ralph had to fight, every day, to fit in, to prove himself worthy, I didn't have to try very hard. And he was *smarter* than me. He was most likely *better* than me. He was certainly *tougher* than me. And funnier.

CLIMBING THE LADDER

Somewhere in these years, in the early to mid-1970s, I heard references to the so-called "American Dream." The metaphor of climbing a "ladder of success" was often employed. I realized that I started a few rungs higher than some people. My skin was white. That's a few rungs—maybe more than a few. My parents were educated. Another rung. My family was middle class. Another. I had some native intelligence, and talent for the kinds of things the world asked of me, without having to put out any effort. Another rung. I was athletic, coordinated, and somewhat graceful. Yet another rung. I am not disabled in any significant way. Another rung. My mom was a teacher and my dad was a preacher, in an era in which such professions were admired. We had status in the community. Another rung.

And then there was the matter of gender, or what we called "biological sex" at the time. It took me even longer to figure this one out than the skin color advantage, but I learned that it mattered that I was *male*. It mattered, a lot. Although the girls I knew certainly had some special advantageous qualities, I learned that the *system* clearly favored boys, boys like me. Some of the clues to this advantage were subtle, like getting called on first or getting better equipment on our side of the playground. Others were more obvious, like when I overheard my ninth grade Algebra teacher tell a female student, "Well, maybe you're just not cut out to do math. Can you cook?" I stood at least a rung above *that* question.

FINDING MY VOICE

During this period, I gained another rung on my ladder. My voice started to change. At first it cracked, but soon it settled into the deeper registers, edging more and more toward bass. Despite my youth, my voice was starting to carry *authority*. I developed a theory: the deeper I pushed my voice, the more everyone seemed to pay attention to what I said. I was emerging as a leader, almost entirely due to the depth and power of my voice. If I spoke somewhat louder and deeper than anyone else, everyone paid attention.

At the time, I was also fascinated with studying the behavior of dogs and developing workable training methods. While laboring to train an extraordinarily headstrong beagle named Jake, I tested my voice theory. The dog snapped to attention. If I hit a high note, he would blithely ignore me, but if I took it down to the bottom, like Sly Stone, he would quickly do as I demanded. I started testing my theory everywhere I went. Sure enough, the deeper registers of my voice proved to be very persuasive. With everyone.

I practiced every day, tuning my instrument. When I moved out west at age 18, I ditched my Southern accent, as I noticed it offered a distinct disadvantage. And I kept on tuning.

Years later, as I became a father and a professor, I started to understand how powerful my voice of authority really was. Is. Although my wife, Susan, and my female colleagues have told me that they are often challenged when they try to assert authority, I can honestly say that it has *never* happened to me, outside of situations in which the other person had higher status or power. Even then, it is rare. When I talk, people *listen*. They rarely, if ever, challenge what I say. My children did this so rarely that I started to worry that they weren't rebellious enough. My students are almost annoyingly compliant.

But I soldier on, because my voice works and because nobody thinks it doesn't. In fact, when I perform my work at academic conferences, my voice is what people compliment most. They like my writing, my use of words, but they *love* my voice.

So, I use it.

I intone the voice of stern authority. People snap to. They do what I want. I am the man in charge. And people listen.

I speak with the voice of the caring father. I am the father figure. I speak with strength, with vigor, with clarity, with authority, with fatherly care. I am the loving, strong, confident father. After all, everyone wants a father like *that*. And people listen.

I speak with the voice of the articulate, hyper-educated, white male professor. I have cultivated this voice over many years of practice. I wear it like an old glove. It is so very natural to me. I know what I'm talking about, or so they believe. And people listen.

I speak with the voice of a lover. I speak softly, invoking and inviting intimacy. My soft voice works too. I am the privileged friend, lover, family member. The soft voice is a powerful persuader. And people listen.

I speak with the voice of the artist. I speak my passion! I am the emotional male, the autoethnographer who writes through his pain. And people listen.

I work my voice and its words like a musical instrument, and it plays well, moving my audience where I want them to go. This white male voice is a finely tuned instrument.

Of course, I've been using this voice for so long that it is a core part of my identity. It is me, and I am it. I am the authority, the father, the professor, the lover, the friend, the artist.

These days, I strive to use my voice, my gift, to improve the world. It all goes back to those early days, when I experienced that convergence of awareness about my starting point on the ladder, and about the power of my gift, my voice, my instrument, to take me closer to the top.

CONCLUSION AND CRITIQUE

Although all this privilege serves my own interests, I sometimes cringe at how easy it all is. After all, it puts the lie to the very opening line of the Declaration of Independence. It turns out that we are *not* all born equal, or at least not with equal privilege. In fact, I was born several rungs up the ladder. I'm not proud of that. This is nothing to be proud of, because I did not earn those rungs. Sure, I earned some of the later ones; I worked hard to get where I am. Getting a Ph.D. and earning tenure, for example, are not easy tasks for anyone. But the deck was stacked in my favor. I started several rungs up the ladder. My privileged position as a white, middle-class male in a white male system was just handed to me.

Still, standing where I stand, not at the very top, but close enough to be aware that I'm ahead of a lot of people, I am aware of my responsibilities. I work every day to help young people find their voices, to speak their truth, their passion, their authority, their hope into being. I want to help them raise questions, to examine injustice and inequality, to stand up for the downtrodden, to engage in deep inquiry, and to live with compassion. I want to help them become people who will work for the greater good, who will be forever infected with humanity, who will always, always, always ask the hard questions and work for better conditions for everyone.

Meanwhile, I hope you, my reader, will start to see your own place in this world, and come to a deeper understanding of how you got where you are. And maybe, just maybe, you will find your voice.

DISCUSSION QUESTIONS

1. Take a moment to reflect upon your own advantages. What advantages or points of privilege do you possess? In other words, what privileged positions (rungs on the ladder) do you occupy? List as many as you can think of.
2. Discuss how you made it to your position in life (your "status"). What challenges or obstacles have you met along the way? How did/will you overcome them?
3. How do you approach people who occupy different status spaces?
4. Discuss the relationships between effort, natural or inborn advantages, and achievement. Do you believe that the "American Dream" is available to everyone in equal measure? Why?

VENUS E. EVANS-WINTERS

5. I AM MY GRANDMOTHER'S CHILD

Becoming a Black Woman Scholar

Pride…If you haven't got it, you can't show it. If you got it, you can't hide it.

(Zora Neale Hurston)

We delight in the beauty of the butterfly, but rarely admit the changes it has gone through to achieve that beauty.

(Maya Angelou)

ROOTS

I was raised within a family and community where there was a strong, dominant female presence. Women in my family were considered beautiful, emotionally and physically strong. Based on Black beauty standards, my mother, grandmother, and aunts sported the right style of clothes, swished from side-to-side the perfect size buttocks, and were always dolled up in the latest hairstyles and wigs. They also had mouths that spewed words of wisdom, cuss words, and jokes as needed. Of course, a woman was even more respected and valued if she was a good cook and homemaker (e.g., tended to the children and elderly, skilled at entertaining company, kept a clean house, etc.). Women who were able to conquer all of the aforementioned areas dominated a "woman's place." Girls in our family took our rightful places too. We were equal to boys – just as strong, just as fast, and just as smart.

Menfolk had their place in the family structure. Men were, for the most part, the breadwinners of the house, and although women definitely had a say and would speak their mind, men had the final say-so on any topic and made it clear that they could throw their weight around if needed. Even though it was known that a man was perfectly capable of physically protecting his family, it was accepted that a woman could protect her family equally as well, with words or any other weapon. Being the man of the house was like holding the trump card, in African American spades vernacular.

P. Leavy (Ed.), Privilege Through the Looking-Glass, 27–33.
© 2017 Sense Publishers. All rights reserved.

The Black girl lived and thrived in a contradictory world – she was recognized, needed, and strong, but her value was always juxtaposed to that of the men around her. Black girls grew up with this juxtaposition in the back of our psyches. We took care of ourselves, we took care of our families, and we were judged on how well we did both. Growing up, I had little care about how White folk viewed me, because I was overly concerned with how other Black women and men sized me up. Was I pretty enough? Was I wife material? Was I able to care for children and the elderly? Was I smart enough, bold enough, and strong enough?

As an adolescent, I began to rebel. The truth was, at least in my mind, I was too skinny and petite to live up to Black standards of beauty. I didn't like the idea of having to take care of bratty children, I did not enjoy cooking or even touching raw food, and I thought men were lazy and women were stupid and weak for taking care of them. By the time high school rolled around, my family determined that I was ruined for marriage. I hated everything related to domestic work and made my feelings very clear. I received a tongue-lashing and backhand or two for my rebellious ways.

Eventually, my family accepted that I was not going to fit into some small, airtight, suffocating box of Black womanhood. They instead pushed me toward education, for they surmised that there was no way a good man would ever take care of me or tolerate my non-domestic and tomboy-ish ways. By high school, I had been introduced to the Civil Rights Movement and Black Nationalism from within my family and popular culture. It was not uncommon for my grandparents to share their own participation or support of the movement.

My maternal grandmother embraced the initiatives of the Black Panthers and was a grassroots activist in Chicago. She advocated and agitated for access to free and affordable housing for the homeless. Grandma and the group she belonged to could not understand why the city of Chicago would allow abandoned houses to accumulate in Black neighborhoods and arrest the transients who sought shelter in them, instead of fixing up the houses and making them suitable, safe shelters for the poor. My paternal grandfather shared stories of my aunt, whom he sent away to college, where she became active in the Black Panther Party against his wishes. Once she began talking about "Back to Africa" politics, he became even more disenchanted with her newfound stance on racial apartheid in the U.S. He was a Korean War veteran who chose different means to address White racism and oppression. He believed in the teachings of Dr. Martin L. King, Thurgood Marshall, and other civil rights leaders.

My grandfather believed that education, voting, and peaceful protests were the path to Black liberation. I believe he thought that I was more like my aunt, but he came to embrace my politics and was my main supporter. My grandmother and an uncle (a former Vietnam veteran, Rastafarian, & activist) introduced the family to Afrocentrism in the late 1980s. Many of our family gatherings, reunions, celebrations, and memorials centered around Africa, Rastafarianism, Black liberation, Black Nationalism, Black spirituality, and ancestral callings. Of all these ancestors, I am my grandmother's child.

FORMS OF EXPRESSION

Those gatherings were simply forms of expression. They made me feel different, or maybe even exotic or extreme in the eyes of my peers. I did not know how those family rituals would later impact my thinking about the social world and how to go about changing it. At the same time, my generation of ghettoized youth was in the midst of a cultural revolution. Hip-hop and gangster rap were introduced to our communities at a time when police harassment and brutality were rampant and the crack cocaine epidemic was plaguing our neighborhoods. We yearned for a war cry.

We yearned for someone or something to explain why everything around us seemed to be falling apart. Families were breaking up; mothers were on crack, brothers were in jail, and fathers were absent. The police were White. Teachers were White. Social workers were White. Doctors were White. Television was White. As a young girl surviving on the block, hip-hop and rap simultaneously represented my rage and my celebration of life. In retrospect, it was also hip-hop that furthered my interest in Black women's empowerment and Black empowerment. Black women's creativity, bodies, and independence were being celebrated alongside calls for a Black consciousness.

Queen Latifah, adorned in Africa attire, called for Black male-female unity. MC Lyte reported in rhyme that she was as strong as a "rock, or I should say a boulder." KRS-One reminded us that "we were headed for self-destruction" if we did not become more conscious to White supremacists' institutions. Public Enemy suggested that we needed to "fight the power" for change. Most radical of all, N.W.A. (Niggaz with Attitude) was sending the message not to trust the police and kill them if necessary.

I was immersed in messages of women's independence, Black unity, and anti-authority teachings. As an adolescent with an impressionable mind, I embraced a Black woman's empowerment standpoint alongside a

29

Black liberation agenda. These two ideologies would certainly influence my identity as a college student, as well as my educational trajectory. Unfortunately, alongside the cries for unity and hope, I also witnessed images of despair, degradation of the Black woman, disparaging images of the Black community, and celebrations of violence and drug and gangster culture.

Poverty and the war on drugs became the harsh reality for many of my family members, neighbors, and classmates. Fortunately, due to the multitude of diverse images, life histories, and familial and cultural teachings that had been impressed onto my psyche, I could concomitantly identify with Black pain, coping, and forms of resistance. This intuitive and cultural ethos became the backdrop for my intellectual pursuits: identifying and naming Black pain, identifying positive and negative coping strategies, and understanding the imperative strategies needed to resist gender, race, and class oppression.

BECOMING...HEAR MY CRY

Many college students, especially first-generation college students from lower-income, working-class, or rural families admit to me that an African American, Latino, or Women's Studies class is what awakened their consciousness to inequality or the marginalization of their communities. In my case, as a younger person, I was inundated with oppression and violence, but simultaneously immersed in emancipatory efforts and acts of Black love and unity.

In the fall of 2014, several doctoral students and young activists I know asked me to list books that have most influenced me for a Facebook challenge. Although I am sure they wanted me to name profound philosophical or historical texts, I purposefully chose books I discovered in my early years that shaped my identity politics. I listed the following books:

1. Roll of Thunder, Hear My Cry (Mildred D. Taylor)
2. Are You There God? It's Me, Margaret. (Judy Blume)
3. Sula (Toni Morrison)
4. Song of Solomon (Toni Morrison)
5. Long Walk to Freedom (Nelson Mandela)
6. Arthur Ashe's biography
7. The Temple of My Familiar (Alice Walker)
8. The Isis Papers: The Keys to the Colors (Dr. Frances Cress Welsing)
9. The Autobiography of Malcolm X
10. No Disrespect (Sister Souljah)

In my early adolescence, I obviously had an affinity for texts that intersected race with gender and location (i.e. Taylor, Morrison, & Souljah). I read *Roll of Thunder, Hear My Cry* in school, borrowed from the school library. My White female teacher thought it was a book I would be interested in reading. I found *Sula* and *Song of Solomon* on the bookshelf in my family's home, next to the encyclopedias. Judy Blume's *Margaret* was the only book I ever read as a child that openly and creatively discussed the questions girls had about puberty, girlhood, maturity, and a girl's relationship to a higher being. Was "He" listening? Interestingly, the female characters in Morrison and Taylor's books were asking similar questions about women's relationship to a spiritual being, but the Black women authors also contemplated a higher being's compassion for women and Black people.

Each of these books, especially in Morrison's style, speak to spirituality or a Black female oneness with the spirit world, but reading *Temple of My Familiar* when I was a new mother rocked my world. I yearned to be the characters in the book. I *was* those characters, and they were me. On that same White teacher's recommendation, I read Nelson Mandela and Arthur Ashe's histories and awakened my consciousness to a contemporary Black struggle. I saw that the Black struggle was not isolated to southern cities in the past; Black people had an ongoing fight against medical, educational, economic, and political apartheid. That teacher does not know that to this day she radicalized me. Yet, through early exposure to books, I became committed to Black liberation because I had associated racialized and gendered faces and stories with the struggle and a set of policies and practices tied to oppression.

By the time I was in college, I had already developed a girl-centered and Black consciousness, due to family experiences, literature, and hip-hop culture. Consequently, in my early college years, I began to seek out cultural spaces and books that further developed and enticed my consciousness. I found Sister Souljah. I was already a fan of Sister Souljah's music when I read her first book. Her ability to connect the Black girl urban experience to larger structural forces showed me how creative writing and storytelling could be used as a medium to reveal how racism and intraracial sexism plays out in Black neighborhoods and relationships. Sister Souljah made the Black experience, despite all of its messiness, consumable and sexy.

Similarly, Malcolm X's biography reminded me that Black men were not helpless victims of their circumstances. His life story reminds any change agent to consider agency alongside of oppression. Radical brothers and sisters always mentioned Frances Cress Welsing's book as a must-read; she blew me away with the *science* behind racism. Ironically, she was the first and only female scientist (not including social scientists) whose work I have ever encountered. I greatly appreciated how she borrowed from biology and physics to explain White racism. *The Isis Papers* was widely read in Black radical circles and shows how science can favor whoever is telling the story. Science is subjective, not only for a Black female author, but for any scientist.

A SCHOLAR'S IDENTITY

I can say in retrospect that for me, the college experience did not initiate my critical consciousness – it was already present in me like a lurking serpent. Instead, college introduced me to the theories behind my gender and racial consciousness. In discussing the intellectual genealogy of Black feminist anthropology, Black feminist scholar McClaurin (2001) explains that, "Most of the contributions to Black Feminist Anthropology are explicit about how their present-day thinking was forged out of a tradition of Black American resistance rooted in the politics, praxis, and poetics of runaway slaves, slave rebellions, Maroons, the underground railroad, slave narratives, Negro spirituals, anti-lynching campaigns, the Civil Rights movement, Black organizations, the Black nationalist movement, the Black Aesthetic, and most recently, reggae and consciousness hip-hop" (p. 4).

Like Black women scholars before me, my identity was forged out of a familial and communal tradition of hearing stories of grandparents born into slavery and working as sharecroppers, introduction to Black history through family storytelling and books, participating in rich Black and African-centered cultural events, and exposure to hip-hop culture. These earlier experiences shaped my worldview and politics and instilled a thirst for a certain type of educational experience and expected outcomes. Finally, the pursuit of higher education would be a time of self-discovery, cultural awareness, and political engagement – a worldview that aligned with my internal self. For me, an education on how to combat racism and sexism and poverty was an education that aligned with my soul.

DISCUSSION QUESTIONS

1. List and discuss a set of books you read in your early years that influenced your viewpoints on race, class, gender, or sexuality. How did these stories shape your identities or help you understand your position in the world (i.e., family, community, or school)?

2. Reflect on your own family experiences from childhood through early adolescence. What experiences or set of experiences most influence your perceptions of who you are as a person and your assumptions about other groups in society?

3. What role did art play in shaping your understanding about the social world? Were there any movies, music, visual art, or television shows that brought you to a level of consciousness or awareness about the world around you? Were these different art forms reflective of your culture or were they significantly different from your lived reality?

4. How might formal education and popular culture intersect to combat power and oppression for individuals and groups?

DONNA Y. FORD

6. ANGRYBLACKSCHOLAR: UNPACKING WHITE PRIVILEGE AS A BLACK FEMALE UNAPOLOGETICALLY CLAIMING AND ASSERTING MY RIGHT TO LIVE MY DREAMS

White privilege denotes unearned advantages that White people have. These include cultural affirmations of their worth, greater social status, and many freedoms at work, play, and speaking. The effects appear in all contexts – educational, professional, social, and personal. White privilege implies the right to assume the universality of one's own experiences, marking others as different or exceptional while perceiving oneself as normal.

Being invited to write this piece required much self-reflection and internal and mental struggle. It is an opportunity to own my anger (and rage) and give some insights into my lived experiences. I do not speak for all or most Black females, but I speak for many. We are righteously angry due to limited privileges, even when we have earned them. What do I know about privilege(s) as a Black female who grew up poor, and who lives in a society rife with racial prejudices and oppression that I experience daily – directly and indirectly? What do I know about privileges when many opportunities for success are snatched from people who look like me? What do I know about privileges when the American Dream seems so elusive to Blacks and some other non-Whites (e.g., Hispanics)? How do I write about privileges as a Black person in the face of affirmative action (what some call 'reverse discrimination')?

Soon after becoming a professor, I read McIntosh's (1990) disquisition on White privilege and appreciated how she unpacked unearned opportunities and advantages as a White person first, and a White female second. Decades later, her list remains relevant. I am ever mindful of denied privileges when selling and purchasing a home or car, searching for the right makeup for my caramel skin, writing checks, seeking to get papers accepted for publication in mainstream journals, and much more. Daily, I witness White privilege

P. Leavy (Ed.), Privilege Through the Looking-Glass, 35–41.

in operation. Whites with higher income and education levels – the status quo – fuel these unearned privileges, feeding social capital in significant and meaningful ways. To wit:

> White skin privilege is not something that white people necessarily do, create, or enjoy on purpose. Unlike the more overt individual and institutional manifestations of racism described above, white skin privilege is a transparent preference for whiteness that saturates our society. White skin privilege serves several functions. First, it provides white people with "perks" that we do not earn and that people of color do not enjoy. Second, it creates real advantages for us. White people are immune to a lot of challenges. Finally, white privilege shapes the world in which we live—the way that we navigate and interact with one another and with the world. (http://www.tolerance.org/article/racism-and-white-privilege)

INTERSECTIONALITY: SO MANY COLLISIONS

I am a Black female; this is a double bind. Crenshaw (1989) concretely and succinctly described "intersectionality" in her essay, "Demarginalizing the Intersection of Race and Sex: A Black Feminist Critique of Antidiscrimination Doctrine, Feminist Theory and Antiracist Politics:"

> Consider an analogy to traffic in an intersection, coming and going in all four directions. Discrimination, like traffic through an intersection, may flow in one direction, and it may flow in another. If an accident happens in an intersection, it can be caused by cars traveling from any number of directions and, sometimes, from all of them. Similarly, if a Black woman is harmed because she is in an intersection, her injury could result from sex discrimination or race discrimination... But it is not always easy to reconstruct an accident: Sometimes the skid marks and the injuries simply indicate that they occurred simultaneously, frustrating efforts to determine which driver caused the harm. (p. 149)

This essay centers on my race more than my gender and other identities. Even with intersectionality in mind, I am a Black person who *happens* to be female more so than a female who happens to be Black. Race is my most salient identity. I see most, if not all, events through a racialized lens. Society taught me to do so. When facing discrimination, my first (and sometimes only) interpretation is that racism is operating more than sexism. Other Black females may feel differently, and that is their right. My lived experiences serve as my frame of reference.

I live in a suburban and mostly White neighborhood. When walking and driving in this expensive community, I worry most about being confronted based on my race, not gender. When shopping, driving, going to the doctor or dentist, teaching, writing, presenting, and more, race more than gender is at the forefront of my concerns. #BlackLivesMatter, #SayHerName, #ShoppingWhileBlack, and #DrivingWhileBlack are all too real. They are more than a hashtag as I go about my daily life as a professor, parent, grandparent, and American citizen. On a recent episode of *Blackish* (January 2017), one of the main actors said it well: "Blacks love America, even though at times America does not seem to love us back".

I will not deny that many people from all walks of life deem me to be very successful and even a role model of both the Protestant work ethic and resilience, but that is relative. I am highly educated (holding a terminal degree), I am currently and have been employed at a prestigious university (several, to be accurate), I have a high income, and I have no criminal record. Still, it is a challenge to enjoy the fruits of my labor with the onslaught of racism in all areas of society. Even if I am not the direct victim or target, so to speak, those who look like me are; I share their pain and anguish – and righteous indignation and rage (Cose, 1994). When I want to celebrate my accomplishments, it is bittersweet. I do not have the "privilege" of enjoying my accomplishments for long when my community – children, students, adults – is suffering and working earnestly to pull themselves up by their proverbial bootstraps. White privilege is a buffer against this anguish, but I am not privy to this. Survival guilt is real and a constant reminder of how defying the odds of social injustices is not easy as I move forward, while looking back (Ford, Davis, Trotman Scott, & Sealey-Ruiz, 2017). In the Black community/ communities, we are often told by parents and elders that, "If you are Black, you have to work two to three times harder than Whites to get ahead, but you may only get half of what they have." This is a function of White privilege, and the myth of meritocracy is in full operation. The irony is that as Whites enjoy their unearned and ignored privileges and advantages, we are told to just pull ourselves up by our bootstraps, and all will be fine.

Everyday decisions that Whites make with barely a thought come with much contemplation for me and other Blacks – ongoing questions of "what if" and "should I." What will Whites think of me if I wear this outfit or hairstyle? What will happen if I say what I really think? How should I phrase that point of view to make it acceptable to Whites? How should I write that manuscript

37

so that the status quo will not reject it? Will my child be respected and valued in that school? Is it safe for me to live in that community/neighborhood? What should I name my child so that he or she will confront less discrimination? People of color, especially Blacks, are penalized for our ethnic names. Employers and educators hold negative and lower expectations when names sound Black, that is, non-White (http://www.huffingtonpost.com/entry/black-sounding-names-study_us_561697a5e4b0dbb8000d687f). Jackie will face higher expectations than Jacqui. James will get a job interview before Jaime. Faculty of color in higher education are the most challenged and disadvantaged when seeking to get their scholarship published; promotion and tenure are greatly compromised. White privilege is operating.

WHITE RACIAL IDENTITY

For some Whites, owning their undeserved privileges is painful and can result in a host of emotions and reactions, such as denial and White guilt. In my experiences, such guilt is too seldom accompanied by relinquishing and sharing, in meaningful ways, the associated unearned benefits. Hardiman's (1982) White Racial Identity Theory, depicted in five stages, is informative, specifically stages 1 and 2. Both *lack of social consciousness*, which includes colorblindness, and *resistance*, which encompasses denial, appear to go hand-in-hand with White privilege.

1. *Lack of Social Consciousness*, characterized by a lack of awareness of racial differences and racism;
2. *Acceptance*, marked by the acceptance of White racist beliefs and behaviors and the unconscious identification with Whiteness;
3. *Resistance*, characterized by the rejection of internalized racist beliefs and messages and rejection of Whiteness;
4. *Redefinition*, characterized by the development of a new White identity that transcends racism; and
5. *Internalization*, marked by the integration of the new White identity into all other aspects of the identity and into consciousness and behavior.

For all racial and ethnic groups, self-knowledge and reflection are essential for a balanced sense of self. One characteristic of White privilege is not having to think about being White. This is elusive to people of color. Daily reminders, such as microaggressions (e.g., Sue, 2010), keep us thinking about being racially different from Whites. For example, only recently can one choose emojis of various skin tones; 90% of children's literature is White (http://blog.leeandlow.com/2015/03/05/the-diversity-gap-in-childrens-publishing-2015/), yet White children represent 52% of PK-12 students; 75% of teachers are White, but 48% of students are not White (Aud et al., 2016). Students of color may never have a teacher who looks like them during their 13 years of formal schooling.

CLASS ACTIVITY – BLACK PRIVILEGE?

For at least 15 years, I have students in one of my college classes read McIntosh's (1990) list of White privileges. The majority students are White females. They check off those privileges that apply to them, and I then ask them to raise their hands based on the frequency of their responses. How many checked 20 or more items? How many checked 15–19 items? … How many checked 0–5? The patterns are consistent: Whites and Asians check most or all, Hispanics and Blacks seldom check more than five.

To end the class activity, I place students in small groups and ask them to create a checklist of school-based privileges for their assigned racial group. They have 15 minutes. The list is extensive from those assigned White privileges (40 or more), and is the same for those assigned Asian privileges. Conversely, the items are few for Hispanic students (10–12) and even fewer for Black students (1–5). When the lists are juxtaposed, reality sinks in. But that is not the end. Students, with my prompting or of their own volition due to class connections and new insights, take notice of patterns. Their notions of privilege for Hispanic students always include having bilingual services and supports for English acquisition. For the record, I inform them that this is an educational right, not a privilege. They find few academic privileges for Black students. The short list always includes an item on affirmative action and athletic scholarships. These are not unearned privileges; affirmative action is necessary to right past and current wrongs. My point: Blacks and Hispanics seldom experience privileges, and the White female students are hard-pressed to find associated privileges for these two groups.

CONCLUSION: RESILIENCE AND GRIT

What Does Mot Kill You Will Make You Stronger

Having shared my lived experiences as a Black female in this short essay, and this is but a slice, I do not view myself as a victim. Pity parties have no room in my life, psyche, and house. Racism is both individual and systemic in society and its institutions (e.g., schools, businesses). I live my life knowing this, but I keep dreaming and pushing boundaries and limits imposed on me by Whites. Adopting a defeatist attitude is counterproductive, and not a privilege that I can afford personally and professionally. I am (rightfully) angry (#AngryBlackWoman), but use this legitimate emotion as motivational fuel to stay the course and to effect change for the most vulnerable, disenfranchised, and oppressed.

In spite of dreams deferred (Langston Hughes) and dreams denied (Ford, 2010, 2013), the story of Black people is one of resilience and grit. We find a way to cope and overcome. Research demonstrates that although White Americans tend to be the "healthiest" racial group, they are also far less resilient than Black Americans. *It seems that vulnerability is a cost of privilege, and resilience comes as a result of adversity.* Whites appear to be more vulnerable to certain psychosocial risk factors (e.g., for a wide range of physical and mental health outcomes) compared to some people of color. In other words, Whites are *less resilient*, less able to successfully adapt to life tasks in the face of highly adverse conditions (https://theconversation.com/black-americans-may-be-more-resilient-to-stress-than-white-americans-62338).

Why are Whites less resilient? One explanation is that, in general, they are not as prepared to cope with adversities because they have less experience dealing with them. This lack of preparedness and experience with stressors may place Whites at the highest risk of poor outcomes when life gets or seems out of control. However, minority groups have consistently lived under economic and social adversities, which has given us firsthand experience and the ability to believe that we can handle the new stressors. For Blacks, a stressor is anything but new. Many of us have mastered coping skills (https://theconversation.com/black-americans-may-be-more-resilient-to-stress-than-white-americans-62338).

In sum, White privilege is a double-edged sword; privilege comes with challenges that few have considered. Racism is not going away, and in fact, seems to be increasing. This nation was built on racism, oppression, and White privilege. Let us learn to work together, with and in spite of our differences. This is a win-win for all.

SUGGESTED RESOURCES

www.culturegrams.com
www.microaggressions.com
http://www.tolerance.org/magazine/archives
https://implicit.harvard.edu/implicit/takeatest.html
http://archive.adl.org/prejudice/print.html

REFERENCES

Cose, E. (1994). *The rage of a privileged class: Why are middle-class Blacks angry? Why should America care?* New York, NY: Harper Perennial.

Crenshaw, K. (1989). Demarginalizing the intersection of race and sex: A Black feminist critique of antidiscrimination doctrine, feminist theory and antiracist politics. *University of Chicago Legal Forum, 1989*(1), 139–167.

Ford, D. Y. (2010). *Reversing underachievement among gifted Black students* (2nd ed.). Waco, TX: Prufrock Press.

Ford, D. Y. (2013). *Recruiting and retaining culturally different students in gifted education.* Waco, TX: Prufrock Press.

Ford, D. Y., Davis, J., Trotman, S. M., & Sealey-Ruiz, Y. (2017). *Gumbo for the soul: Liberating memoirs and stories to inspire females of color.* Charlotte, NC: Information Age Publishing.

Hardiman, R. (1982). *White identity development: A process oriented model for describing the racial consciousness of White Americans* (Doctoral dissertation). Retrieved from ProQuest. (No. AAI8210330)

Kena, G., Hussar, W., McFarland, J., de Brey, C., Musu-Gillette, L., Wang, X., Zhang, J., Rathbun, A., Wilkinson-Flicker, S., Diliberti, M., Barmer, A., Bullock, M. F., & Dunlop, V. E. (2016). *Condition of education 2016.* Washington, DC: U.S. Dept. of Education, National Center for Education Statistics. Retrieved from https://nces.ed.gov/programs/coe/

McIntosh, P. (1990). White privilege: Unpacking the invisible knapsack. *Independent School, 49*(2), 31–35. Retrieved from http://people.westminstercollege.edu/faculty/jsibbett/readings/White_Privilege.pdf

Sue, D. (2010). *Microaggressions in everyday life: Race, gender, and sexual orientation.* New York, NY: Wiley.

LIZA TALUSAN

7. MY RESPONSIBILITY TO CHANGE

I grew up anti-Black.

The kid in me wants to believe it was unintentional. The well-intentioned and educated grown-up in me wants to believe it's not true. The human being who wakes up each day to violence perpetuated against people who are Black knows that it is all too real.

To be a person in the United States (because that's the only place I have grown up) means that I have grown up anti-Black. From the moment I came into this world, I was told how pretty my "light skin" was. I was advised not to spend too much time out in the sun because I "shouldn't get too dark."

I grew up singing childhood songs that used the n*word. I believed that all princess were White and worthy of rescuing. I believed that to be American was to be White, with those words "White" and "American" used interchangeably throughout my life. No one ever told me differently. No one ever told me that there were other ways to be beautiful. No one ever told me that there were other cultures that were strong, mighty, and leaders.

When I was in middle school, 12 years old, my friend introduced me to the music of Ziggy Marley. She knew every single word to every single song. She played the compact disc in her stereo over and over again, making us wonder if the repeat button was, in fact, stuck. To be friends with Jenny (*name has been changed) meant that you, too, knew every single word to every single Ziggy Marley song. So, it came as no surprise that she wanted to be Ziggy Marley for Halloween. She grabbed a boombox, popped the CD into the case, and prepared to bring it to school. She found clothing with bright colors. She also bought dark foundation from the local CVS and carefully painted her pale, White skin. We twisted her light-brown hair using excessive amounts of gel. When we arrived at school, everyone celebrated her costume and the lengths at which she went to "be Ziggy." None of our teachers or other adults told her to remove the makeup. No one explained the practice of blackface, and certainly no one told her that this was offensive. We never learned about a time in history when blackface was used as an exclusionary practice against Black actors. We never critically examined,

P. Leavy (Ed.), Privilege Through the Looking-Glass, 43–48.

through film, readings, or discussions about cultural appropriation, the ways in which White people exaggerated features of Black people or Black culture. My education and upbringing was, essentially, void of any context about people of color.

Growing up in a nearly all-White town, I only knew two girls who are Black during my entire time in kindergarten through high school. I did not have a relationship with them other than a brief shared stint as cheerleaders in sixth grade or a bus ride on a student council trip in seventh grade. I was in honors history and English classes, went to a well-resourced public school, and was active in town sports. My interactions were solely with White children, peers, families, coaches, and teachers.

In school, my curriculum reflected the identities of my peers. We spent an entire semester studying the industrial roots of my hometown, the traditional (White) journey through both European and United States AP History, and read the foundational English books by White men. If we talked at all about people of color, it was to impress upon us that people who are Black were slaves. In music class, we sang field songs without any historical or racial context about violence or salvation.

Every February, I learned about Harriet Tubman, Martin Luther King, and Rosa Parks, but never about Malcolm X or any leaders from racial backgrounds other than White. In fact, the first time I ever heard about Malcolm X was when the movie *Malcolm X* was released in theaters. It was late in my senior year of high school, and all of my friends said, "My parents told me not to go to the movies when *Malcolm X* is playing because all the Black people are gonna try to beat us up after it's done."

I didn't see the film until my senior year in college, four years after its theater release. It had finally come out on a VHS tape and, still impacted by the fear perpetuated by my peers, I watched it alone in my dorm room. I still have that double VCR tape sitting in a box in my living room.

It wasn't until my college years that I developed meaningful relationships with people who are Black. For the first time, I heard about W.E.B. Du Bois, Alice Walker, Zora Neale Hurston, Toni Morrison, Angela Davis, bell hooks, and Cornel West. Their names were strangers to me, but for some of my peers, these were their foundational texts. They had their pictures framed on shelves in their homes. They drew from the strength of strong writers and intellectuals to inform their own Black identity and experience.

As a storyteller and writer, I'm left wondering: have you read this first part of my story and thought about who I am racially? Given my statements, experiences, and reflections, did you assume I was White? What does that assumption say about race and racialized experiences? What does that assumption mean about the juxtaposition of race?

Well, I'm not White. I am Asian American.

"What? How can that be? How can you be a person of color and grow up anti-Black?" you might be wondering.

That's the interesting thing about race and racism, isn't it? That's the interesting thing about power and privilege. That's the interesting thing about education and experience.

I believe that to grow up in the United States of America means growing up in an anti-Black system, regardless of your own racial identity. In many ways, our schooling, our curriculum, our experiences, the media, stereotypes, and lack of interaction inform our beliefs. It is important to know that, individually, many Black families have taken on the responsibility of providing culturally relevant and responsive lessons because of the lack of responsibility in our schools. In my own upbringing, people who were White always had their cultures affirmed through our curriculum, our teachers, and our leaders. For people of color, these "windows and mirrors" are largely missing.

But times are changing. We are holding schools – higher education, included – more accountable for educating our communities to be culturally responsible, responsive, and reflective. We've seen a (re)emergence of literature and films around the issues of racism that continue to impact people and communities who are Black. It is no wonder that books like *The New Jim Crow* by Michelle Alexander, *Between the World and Me* by Ta-Nehisi Coates, and *Just Mercy* by Bryan Stevenson have become required reading in the past few years. Just this year alone, we have engaged in intense dialogue about *13th* by Ava DuVernay or the film *I Am Not Your Negro* (based on the work of James Baldwin) by Raoul Peck. Historically, we have always drawn attention to the differences in Black experiences in this country. We have also witnessed pushback to transformative movements like #BlackLivesMatter with false efforts to include all lives.

Even as a person of color, as a daughter of immigrants, and as a frequent recipient of racist questions ("Where are you *really* from?"), I, too, am a product of a country that has reduced the experiences of people and communities who identify as Black to singular stories. My responsibility to dismantle, disrupt, and defy these systems is exactly why I have written this essay.

If I am to acknowledge any privilege in my life, it is the privilege to recognize when I have failed.

I am angry that, some days, I convince myself that it is not my fault that I grew up in an environment that was so rooted in stereotyping people who are Black. In my head, some days, I say, "Well, it's not *my fault* that I grew up that way," or, "It's not *my fault* that my teachers didn't teach me about race," or, "It's not *my fault* there were only two Black families in our town."

It is not my fault, but the consequences are my responsibility.

I grow even angrier when I realize that a system of supremacy created these feelings, beliefs, and experiences for me. Through ignorance and/ or intention, the stories of powerful Black people were left out of my development, education, and upbringing while the stories of slavery and dependence limited my understanding of the richness and complexities of Black cultures. "Pull yourself up by your bootstraps" and "If you try hard, you can be anything" echoed in my hallways. The warnings of fear and mistrust were the foundation for avoiding relationships and creating distance.

And, I grow even angrier when I admit that, as a fellow person of color who has worked to ally closer with the Black community, anti-Blackness is part of my narrative.

Throughout my adulthood, I have relentlessly worked to change this approach in my own schooling through my work as an educational leader and practitioner and through my scholarship. I am heavily involved in curriculum reform to more accurately center stories of people of color. I work closely with faculty and teachers who accept responsibility for diversifying their curriculum. As a parent, I have open conversations with my children. Their young lives have been filled with dialogue and experiences about race, about the beauty of Blackness and the parts they self-identify as their heritage, and we work to educate people in my age group and generation about how we grew up. Together, we read books, discuss controversial topics in the news and media, and talk openly about the experiences of their friends who identify as Black. I challenge and push them to truly acknowledge what it means to be an ally to friends who are Black. I challenge them to identify a real plan for what they will or can do if they are witnesses to anti-Blackness. I remind them of both the privileges and challenges we face as an Asian American and an Asian-Latino family.

As an Asian American, I own that my own community has had problematic approaches to race, both in ways we have been accepted and in ways we have been excluded in America. I have grown to understand just how my own community was, through systems of Whiteness, set up to be anti-Black. Through hyped-up media and aggregated data, my very identity as an Asian American was pitted against Blackness by reducing the struggles and successes of dozens of ethnic groups into one singular "Asian American" experience. I was told I was privileged and given privileges. I was taught that people who are Black were so different from me. I believed I was *me* and they were *those people.*

I grew up with messaging that was so toxic and poisonous that I am required to check these biases every single day. I do this because I have the privilege to forget. I check my privilege every single day when I look into the eyes of my husband and his family who, through complicated histories of Puerto Rico, run shades from light to dark. I check it every single day when I brush out the tightly curled hair of my oldest child, feeling strands wrap around my fingers in ways that my own straight, smooth, flat hair does not. I check it when I tell my son, "No, I will not buy you that toy gun, even the one that looks like a neon play thing" out of fear that he will be in our front yard when someone calls to report him to the police.

I check it every single day when I wake up. I check it every single day when I go to bed.

I remind myself that, growing up in the context of the United States, I am a product of anti-Blackness through education and socialization. I am reminded of my responsibility to change this for myself, for others, and for the many voices that go unheard. #BlackLivesMatter

DISCUSSION QUESTIONS

1. What were your first messages about privilege? Where did you learn about privilege?
2. Dr. Talusan centers her narrative on how she learned, and didn't learn, about communities and/or people who are Black. What were your first or earliest messages about communities and/or people who are Black? Were these messages positive, negative, or neutral?
3. Learning comes from both formal and informal experiences. Turn and talk with a partner about the formal (e.g., school, books, articles, movies, documentaries) ways you learned about race and the informal (e.g., conversations with friends, television, messages about value or importance, social media) ways you learned about race.
4. Dr. Talusan writes about times when she experiences privileges based on her racial identity as an Asian American and how she also experiences marginalization based on her identity. Our different identities are often privileged or often marginalized at different times, in different situations, and in different contexts. How have you experienced privilege or

marginalization based on the different aspects of your identity?

5. Dr. Talusan gives a few examples of how, every day, she is reminded that she has to change. One way is that she identifies as an ally to people who are Black. People often use the phrase, "I'm an ally to _____ community." Identify a community that you say you ally with, and write down the ways in which you make that actionable. Share out with a partner or small group that is also developing ally behavior with that same or similar community.

VIDEO CLIPS ABOUT PRIVILEGE

The Unequal Opportunity Race (https://www.youtube.com/watch?v=vX_Vzl-r8NY).
Buzzfeed's What Is Privilege (https://www.youtube.com/watch?v=hD5f8GuNuGQ).

SUGGESTED RESOURCES

Harvard University's Project Implicit Test (https://implicit.harvard.edu/implicit/takeatest.html).
Mahzarin Banaji, Ph.D. and Anthony Greenwald, Ph.D. *Blindspot: Hidden Biases of Good People.*

AMY L. MASKO

8. BLACK HERE, OBURNI THERE

Differentials in Race and Privilege in the
United States and West Africa

Borɔnyi, Borɔnyi How Are You? We Are Fine, Thank You. And You?

This melodic chant followed us around the city of Cape Coast, Ghana, sung by school children to greet us whenever we passed. We typically answered this call with the expected sung response, "We are fine, thank you," which was almost always followed by a sea of giggles, and then school children swarming us to walk, chat, and hold our hands through town, as if we were rock stars.

My husband and I moved our family to Cape Coast for one year, where my children attended elementary school and we attempted to integrate into the fabric of the community. My husband and I are both White and all four of our children are African American. Our family is formed through adoption and would be classified as transracial or interracial. The two terms are used interchangeably in adoption; the prefix trans- means "across, beyond, through," and the prefix inter- means "between, among, mutually, reciprocally, together." I prefer the term interracial, as it fits the view of my family as "among" rather than "across." However, trans- is the prefix most often used with adoption, which indicates that the children really do not have a say in the mutuality of the relationship, whereas inter- is the prefix most often used with relationships, indicating that two people consent to be in a mutually beneficial, reciprocal relationship. As my children have aged to nearly all be teenagers now, I believe we have evolved from a transracial family, where my husband and I chose to adopt children with a different ethnic background from ourselves, to an interracial family, where we live and love together, among each other, with mutual feelings of familial bonds. However, I recognize that my husband and I live with unearned privileges granted to us due to our race, privileges that my children are not granted. In this way, we experience a separation of lived experience that perhaps will never allow us

P. Leavy (Ed.), Privilege Through the Looking-Glass, 49–55.

to truly be "among" each other. In this way, the social construct of race in the United States is so profound that it essentially gives members of the same family different lived experiences. This essay will document my experience as a White mother of four African American children, specifically as our family life relates to race, power, and privilege, by examining the social construction of these elements and how they have changed and transformed throughout our lived experiences here in the United States and abroad in Ghana, West Africa. I will discuss the positionality, power, and privilege as it relates to race in an American and West African context, highlighting the intersection of these concepts, suggesting that while statuses change based on historical, geopolitical, and sociocultural contexts, the intersection with power is a static element.

As a White woman, I have the privilege of not having to think about race and racism on a daily basis. In fact, I rarely have to think about it all. I went through most of my life thinking about racism only when I wanted to, and always in terms of social justice; I wanted to live in and work toward a more just, kind, and gentle society that supported racial equity. I wrote papers about it in college, when I was studying to be a teacher. I worked to be a multicultural educator, taking every opportunity to attend workshops and trainings about diversity. However, I was always an outside observer to the experiences of racism. I was never once forced to grapple with racism; I only engaged if I wanted to. I did want to and shaped my career to work in urban schools and chose to live in a diverse neighborhood in the city. So, I chose to engage with racism, but I never *had* to, and even when I did, I did so as an outsider, as an ally, perhaps, but not as a person who experiences racial oppression. Peggy McIntosh (1988; 1995) describes this White privilege in her famous list of 46 privileges that White people experience. Below are two that perfectly describe my experience:

1. I can, if I wish, arrange to be in the company of people of my own race most of the time. (p. 77–78)

34. I can worry about racism without being seen as self-interested or self-seeking. (p. 77–78)

DiAngelo (2011) further explains the phenomenon: "White people in North America live in a social environment that protects and insulates them from race-based stress. This insulated environment of racial protection builds white expectations for racial comfort" (p. 54). These two scholars effectively described my lived experience of White privilege until I became the mother of an African American baby girl. At that point I was forced to confront racism on a nearly daily basis.

My Black children have experienced racism. My son had a White friend tell him in the fourth grade that he should only play with Black kids on the playground. My sons both get more fouls called on them on the basketball court and soccer field than their White peers, even when their peers commit more fouls. Apparently, they appear to play with more aggression. My daughter's teacher told me that regardless of her nearly perfect report card, she was having a lot of problems at school that needed remediation: a therapy group at lunch to work on conflict management, speech therapy because she was difficult to understand, and a recommendation for ADHD medication. Another time, a teacher told me that my seventh grade son, who was taking honors-level Science, should reconsider taking honors Biology in the eighth grade because it would be hard for him. He had a 99% A in the class. When I asked the teacher why he made such a recommendation, he vaguely responded that he just thought my son would struggle and there were some kids he believed should rethink the honors course for eighth grade. I did not ask him if all of the kids on this list were of color, but I should have. We have consistently ignored all the academic limits that teachers have placed on our children over the years. We are keenly aware of the institutionalized and structural racism within schools and do our best to make decisions with this context front and center in our minds.

We have also experienced discrimination as an interracial family. There are people who do not agree with or support interracial adoption. While I will not label this discrimination as racism, it is still race-based and sometimes difficult to navigate. Many African American women have approached me to critique how I have styled my daughter's hair, for example, or to caution me that it is difficult to raise Black boys in this society and challenge my competence in doing so. We have been denied the bathroom once, which I suspect was because the African American salesperson did not approve of a White woman with a Black child. We have heard countless thoughtless comments about our family. Yet in these situations, I still am a person of privilege, which is why it cannot be labeled as racism. Racism is discrimination plus power. When we were denied the bathroom, I approached a manager, complained about the salesperson, and was provided the key to the bathroom. I have been raised with power and agency. I was raised by society to believe that I can get things done, and as Peggy McIntosh (1988, 1995) describes with number 33 on her list: "My culture gives me little fear of ignoring the perspectives and powers of people of other races" (p. 78).

   The American context has provided my family with a landscape that suggests my children are not as capable as White children, are more aggressive than White children, are not as articulate as White children, and should limit themselves to friendships with children who look like them. The people who have interacted with my family in these racist ways would not describe themselves as racist. In fact, they may not be. These may not be racist teachers and referees and children, but they are operating in normative ways in a hegemonic society that consistently tells them with insidious messages that they should fear Black boys, that African American speech is inarticulate, and that African American children do not fare well in school. "Hegemony is the process through which we learn to see the social narratives that support the interests of those in power – oligarchies and plutocracies – as normal, natural, and commonsense, even when they do not equate with our interests" (Lea, 2014, p. 185). So, while these may or may not be examples of personal racism, they are examples of hegemony. Race is a social construct that has no biological truth to it, yet operates in powerful ways that provide very different life opportunities and lived experiences for people of color.

   When my oldest daughter was in fifth grade and my youngest was in kindergarten, we moved our family to Cape Coast, Ghana for the year. I taught at the university there and conducted ethnographic research on village schooling practices. Our children attended elementary school and we all engaged with Ghanaian society and culture in a multitude of different ways. When the Chief International Officer at my university asked me why I wanted to apply for a Fulbright scholarship to Ghana, one of my responses was that I wanted to understand how race was socially constructed, and is therefore understood and experienced differently in different parts of the world. In this way, I wanted to understand positionality more deeply. The idea of positionality is not that people are defined by a fixed set of traits, but rather by their location within a shifting network of relationships. Understanding positionality suggests that I might better understand where one stands in relation to power. I research race and schooling in the U.S., and my argument was that this global experience would help me understand the American context of the social construction of race more deeply, in turn making me a better researcher. In reality, I wanted that understanding for my children. I wanted this international experience so they would be better able to cope with the hegemonic society in which they live. I actually did not know how race was constructed in Ghana. I did not know what to anticipate about their treatment or our treatment, but I was confident that we would all come to new understandings about race after living in a West African country for a year, and as a result, they would grow up with a greater ability to weather the racist American context.

It came as a surprise that my children were referred to as *borɔnyi* in Ghana. *Borɔnyi* is the Fante term for "white person."[1] My children expected their father and me to be the minority. They expected to be in the majority and for us to experience some of what they experience in their daily lives. We even joked about it before we left. My fifth grader was looking forward to it! However, in Ghana what mattered more than skin color was a geopolitical identity as a Westerner. We were all American, all from the West. We were all "from beyond the horizon" (Botchway, 2008). For Ghanaians, this translated, even if not literally, at least socioculturally, as "white." In fact, the term *borɔnyi* was used interchangeably with "white," even when referring to my dark-skinned children. And this geographic and political positionality came with unearned privileges. It came with a social status that was mostly venerated, but also sometimes abhorred.

Ghana is a postcolonial context, and as such has a complex relationship with the West. Until 1957, Ghana was a British colony, which means it is a fairly young country (albeit the first in Africa to gain its independence). For centuries Ghana was a main port of the Trans-Atlantic Slave Trade, where 12.5 million Africans were shipped as cargo to the Americas. After the slave trade ended in 1807, Ghanaians spent another 150 years under British colonial rule. And while the colonial era is officially over, the neo-colonial era is not. The term neo-colonial was coined by Dr. Kwame Nkrumah, the first president of Ghana, who argued that this new form of colonialism, executed by financial control of the emerging economies of newly independent nations was more insidious and more difficult to detect than classic colonialism (Ashcroft, Griffiths, & Tiffin, 2007). Nyikal (2005) agrees, arguing that,

> …colonialism is not over as such. There is merely a new form of colonialism, by the same western countries, masked under the pretext of economic support for Africa, directly enforced or institutionalized in the World Bank, the International Monetary Fund (IMF) and the World Trade Organization (WTO). The policies enforced on poor African countries through these organizations have chained Africa to continued dependence on western economies for mere subsistence, by preventing self help to the continent's economic problems. Moreover, the same policies seem to favor a trade imbalance to the already wealthy Western economies over the struggling ones in Africa. This economic colonization of Africa has done and continues to do as much damage to the continent as the imperial colonialism and its after effects did. (p. 1)

53

It is in this context that Westerners are both loved and hated. It is this tension that my family came to understand privilege and positionality on another level within another set of circumstances. "Colonialism, racism, and Whiteness are hegemonic processes" (Lea, 2014, p. 185), and in Ghana we were all part of the hegemony. Our position as Westerners was one of power. We were part of the neo-colonial class, even if we did not understand that we directly benefited from our position. We were adored because we were Americans. We were from a nation that held superpower status, politically, but also culturally. Our country produced Hollywood films and was home to Beyoncé and Michael Jackson. Barack Obama was our President. Cape Coast claimed the moniker "Obama City" when President Obama visited in 2008. My oldest son was called Obama because "one day he will grow up to be a great leader." Our position was that of privilege.

The legacy of the slave trade is the resulting low status of African Americans on the racial hierarchy in the United States, and the elevated one of White Americans. The legacy of colonialism has produced a similar racial hierarchy, although status is granted based on your geopolitical context, whether you are African or Western. There is an intersection of power and privilege as they relate to race in an American and West African context. In order for one group to have privilege, another must be oppressed. While my children's statuses change based on historical, geopolitical, and sociocultural contexts, the intersection of privilege with power is a static element.

DISCUSSION QUESTIONS

1. The author suggests that living in Ghana might better equip her children to cope with racism in the United States. Explore that idea, in terms of positionality. How might the idea of positionality influence their understanding of racism as they grow up?
2. How does this article help you to understand the notion of "racial hierarchy?" Is the hierarchy static or can ethnic groups move up and down the hierarchy? What influences the dynamic or static position on the racial hierarchy?
3. The author claims that statuses change based on various sociological and political factors, but that power remains a constant. In what ways does power remain static?
4. Racism is defined in this article as discrimination plus power. Is it possible for a white person to experience racism in the context of the United States?

NOTE

[1] *Borɔnyi* is the Fante term used for whites, visitors, Europeans. It is a word that appears in various forms in all of the indigenous languages spoken in Ghana. Ghanaian linguists put forth three arguments as to the etymology of the term: (1) a person from beyond the horizon/far away, (2) people of the maize, perhaps comparing the trait of straight hair to the silk of the maize cob, or (3) a wicked person who mistreated me. Botchway (2008) argues that since many of the other languages in Ghana have a definition most similar to the third argument, it is possibly the origin of the Fante term, *borɔnyi*, as well (Botchway, 2008).

REFERENCES

Ashcroft, B., Griffiths, G., & Tiffins, H. (2007). *Post-colonial studies: The key concepts* (2nd ed.). New York, NY: Routledge.

Botchway, D. N. Y. M. (2008). When the people decide: Colonialism, social and economic changes and the emergence of modern nationalist in the Gold Coast. *Journal of Faculty of Arts, 1*(1), 168–217.

DiAngelo, R. (2011). White fragility. *International Journal of Critical Pedagogy, 3*(3), 54–70.

Lea, V., & Edouard-Gundowry, M. S. (2014). Targeted by the crosshairs: Student voices on colonialism, racism, and whiteness as barriers to educational equity. In A. I. Steinberg & S. R. Steinberg (Eds.), *Critical youth studies reader* (pp. 184–194). New York, NY: Peter Lang Publishing, Inc.

McIntosh, P. (1988/2015). White privilege and male privilege: Unpacking the invisible knapsack. In M. L. Anderson & P. H. Collins (Eds.), *Race, class, & gender: An anthology* (9th ed., pp. 74–78). Belmont, CA: Wadsworth Publishing.

Nyikal, H. (2005). *Neo-colonialism in Africa: The economic crisis in Africa and the propagation of the status quo by the world bank/IMF and WTO* (Unpublished manuscript). Palo Alto, CA: Stanford University.

MAYME LEFURGEY

9. BUYING A BETTER WORLD?
THE INTERSECTIONS OF CONSUMERISM,
CLASS, AND PRIVILEGE IN GLOBAL
WOMEN'S RIGHTS ACTIVISM

INTRODUCTION

Many global campaigns exist that seek to raise awareness about women's issues, including girls' education, reproductive rights, violence against women, and pay equity. These activist efforts and their narratives can be found on billboards, television screens, in magazines, and through various social media outlets. You may know these campaigns and projects, and in some cases, have participated in them through clubs, educational institutions, or social networks. They may have a particular message they want to promote or a central idea they want participants to mobilize forward. For example, supporters may be asked to create an event of their own, wear a wristband or t-shirt to show support, or be called on to buy or sell products to raise awareness or funds. The motivation to unite women across the globe through these initiatives is easily understandable, given how many of these women's issues are widespread and affect women around the world and across cultural lines. There is certainly an ever-present need for collective activism, awareness, and fundraising for the many causes connected to women's lived experiences.

When critically analyzing some of these initiatives, however, it is possible to uncover some contentions with the good intentions that are at play. Some campaigns and projects, despite their motivation to fight for and forge equality, may actually unintentionally contribute to inequality and reinforce global power dynamics, hindering opportunity for solidarity and effective activism. In this chapter, I will focus specifically on issues of class privilege and consumerism and how they influence, and in some cases, detract from the aims of global women's rights activism. In order to better understand this reality, I will engage with feminist theorist and lawyer Kimberlé Crenshaw's notion of intersectionality as a conceptual framework to unpack some of the tensions and shortcomings within international women's rights organizing.

P. Leavy (Ed.), Privilege Through the Looking-Glass, 57–63.

DEVELOPING AN INTERSECTIONAL UNDERSTANDING

An intersectional analysis acknowledges the complex power relations between various identity markers, including but not limited to gender, race, class, sexuality, ability, and nationality. Intersectionality offers the potential for a more thorough and critical analysis that accounts for different layers and dimensions of a person's identity. Intersectionality as a lens has sought to expose "single-axis thinking," or narrow, one-dimensional thinking, which can discount a variety of possibilities and undermine the broader struggle for social justice and the attainment of women's rights globally (Cho, Crenshaw, & McCall, 2013). In her trailblazing paper, *Mapping the Margins: Intersectionality, Identity Politics, and Violence against Women of Color,* Crenshaw discusses research she conducted at a women's shelter and the dynamics of intersectionality she observed during this project.

> The physical assault that leads women to these shelters is merely the most immediate manifestation of subordination they experience. Many women who seek protection are unemployed or underemployed, and a good number of them are poor. Shelters serving these women cannot afford to address only the violence inflicted by the batterer; they must also confront the other multilayered and routinized forms of domination that often converge in these women's lives hungering their ability in create alternatives to abusive relationships that brought them to the shelters in the first place. (Crenshaw, 1991, p. 1245)

As we learn from this example, intersectionality sheds light on the ways in which realities of gender, race, class, and other identity categories intersect and impact the lives of women, including their advocacy and work. The wide-ranging applicability of intersectionality allows for a more thoughtful analysis of the complex lived realities of women across various cultural, geographic, and political contexts. Engaging intersectionality in the analysis of global women's rights campaigns offers the opportunity to look beyond categories of gender alone and includes other aspects of the lived identities of women.

To speak briefly from personal experience, when working abroad as a Gender Specialist, it was easy for me to buy in to the trope that "any help was better than none." My colleagues and I failed to recognize the very serious and often damaging implications of international aid and development work, both on local communities and global power dynamics. I later gained a more nuanced perspective and realized that what might work in my country or community might not apply elsewhere, reinforcing the notion that there is no one-size-fits-all approach to advocating for women's rights. This experience also increased my awareness about the need to see beyond the duality of gender and to consider other aspects of women's lives that intersect. Similarly, when first introduced to the foundations of feminist theory and activism during my undergraduate studies, I became increasingly interested in learning about women's rights campaigns and sought out opportunities to support them. I joined clubs, donated to campaigns, raised awareness on social media, and often bought products that supported these causes, such as jewelry and clothing. My initial thought was that this system was win-win. I could purchase a product I wanted *and* contribute to broader goals for gender equality. What I have since learned is that the reality is not so simple, and these types of initiatives, despite their best intentions, can have unintended consequences and may actually be contributing to harmful global dynamics that hinder women's equality. In my experience, intersectionality has been an important tool in helping me to understand very complex global dynamics. It has aided in acknowledging my own privilege and the ways in which my efforts to help and advocate may have had unintended consequences due to a lack of understanding of broader dynamics. I will now use a few campaigns as examples to further explain the complexities I describe.

EXAMINING GLOBAL CAMPAIGNS

First, it is important to briefly make note of a recent trend in international advocacy of all kinds (not only gender-based activism) that sells the ideals of global human rights activism through consumerism (Daley, 2013). There are increasing opportunities for people to engage through consumer-powered projects and campaigns than ever before. Some scholars have argued that this reality may allow for supporters to disengage from the more political aspects of a campaign by offering a quick sense of gratification from purchasing wristbands, ribbons, t-shirts, and other such products (Richey & Ponte, 2011). This allows consumers to feel as though they are contributing to social change while actually contributing to an often-harmful system of global economic exchange and, in some cases, the exploitation of those making the products. Against this backdrop, creative pitches sell products to those who can afford them – supporters who often live in what is deemed "developed," "western" or Global-North societies – and these groups of privileged individuals provide little in the way of activist efforts beyond this exchange.

We can look to projects like the signature RED products sold by corporations such as Apple, Starbucks, and Gap for HIV/AIDS awareness and fundraising. Similarly, Tom's Shoes' "One for One" campaign donates a pair of shoes or glasses to someone in need with every purchase made (Red, 2014; Tom's Shoes, 2014). Sevenly promotes a different charity each week, selling T-shirts for $30, while donating $7 to the featured organization (Sevenly, 2014). The website tracks the number of fundraising dollars contributed by purchasers, as well as tallies "the number of people helped" by the campaign with the overall aim to inspire "a generation of generosity" (Sevenly, 2014). This dynamic raises several critical questions, such as: Who consumes the products and who works in factories to make them? How does this relationship, which relies on consumerism as activism, work towards effective societal change?

Many campaigns say that they are working to "empower" women through increasing their rights and ending violence against them. For example, the Nomi Network is an initiative that sells clothing and purses to "save women from trafficking" with their popular "Buy Her Bag, Not Her Body" and "Buy Her Shirt, Not Her Body" campaigns (Nomi Network, 2014). Trades of Hope focuses on jewelry, which translates women's poverty in the Global South into "purposeful entrepreneurial opportunities for the modern American woman through the selling of fashion accessories and home décor" (Trades of Hope, 2014a). This campaign in particular draws on the theme of a "global sisterhood" in their visual marketing campaign to "give women a better life," while helping to change "stories of pain and struggle to a story of hope" (Trades of Hope, 2014b). Yet with a quick look at their marketing, the sisterhood appears to be among the American buyers and not among women involved in the project from other regions.

APPLYING INTERSECTIONALITY

Though the projects I have mentioned vary in product, target region, or social issue, they all tell a similar narrative of a *helped* and *helper* divide, and bring into serious question the politics of philanthropy (King, 2004; Youde, 2009). They challenge what it means to work collaboratively across cultural and geographic lines and call for a nuancing of the aims of consumerism-driven global feminist work. The projects I have described have great marketing and thoughtful mission statements. One might argue that, in some respects, such initiatives work to challenge the ways people consume and offer alternative companies to support within the broader market of purchasing goods.

60

However, this model of activism can also depoliticize structural barriers that most hinder the progression of women's rights by promoting individualized, market-based solutions to problems that, in actuality, require major policy and societal changes. In navigating these campaign messages and products, it is imperative to differentiate passionate subscriptions to causes and the actual changes that these campaigns produce in the world. A key aspect of this is a commitment to uncovering and understanding the ways in which advocates and organizations can be implicated in the injustices they seek to address (Mahrouse, 2014). For example, consumer-driven campaigns can be negligent of the global dynamics of consumerism that leave some women in factories creating campaign materials and others with the agency to participate in "activism" by buying the necessary products (Bair, 2010). Even with the best of intentions, problematic relationships to global capitalist ventures exist that are often not in the best interest of women's rights or liberation, given that consumerism is largely fueled by patriarchal and capitalist entities that are concerning to feminists (Mohanty, 2003).

Feminist theorist Chandra Mohanty reinforces this idea when she writes that "radical theory can in fact become a commodity to be consumed; no longer seen as a product of activist scholarship or connected to emancipatory knowledge" and, rather, can act as a sign of prestige and privilege, creating a complex landscape of inequality (2013, p. 971). Mohanty outlines the need to not only analyze capitalism and class as global realities in our critiques of corporations and institutions, but also within our social movements and within women's rights activism (Mohanty, 2013). With this, we learn that gender-based concerns cannot be separated from the realities of global consumption patterns, and their embedded inequalities are from norms of social class that allow some to participate over others and reinforce systems of hierarchy.

As consumers in an increasingly globalized world, it is crucial to be aware of the ways in which social justice messages are translated into easily consumable messages and products that "refashion contemporary humanitarianism as an empathetic gesture of commoditized concern" and can overshadow structural issues contributing global inequality (Mostafanezhad, 2014, p. 112). This simplification can also delegitimize other forms of activism that require more thoughtful commitment, education, and attention beyond the quick fix and instant gratification of buying products which purport values of equality.

In conclusion, global women's movements and campaigns can and do represent the urgent need to bring attention to women's rights issues across the globe. These campaigns have the ability to act as vehicles for social justice and can be outlets for genuine partnership and solidarity across difference. It is important to understand and look critically upon such initiatives and our role within them, while working to address their limitations in adequately advocating for equality, which requires us to go beyond categories of gender alone. Although the motivations, both among consumers and within the organizations they support, are often good and seek to include women globally, a more critical analysis is warranted in order to understand the far-reaching implications of activism. This critical reflection allows for a more thoughtful dialogue on privilege and can more accurately reflect the deeply complex, intersectional nature of global women's rights campaigns, including the various ways women participate in them and are affected by them.

DISCUSSION QUESTIONS

1. Who coined the term intersectionality and what does it mean?
2. How do you understand intersectionality in your own life? Can you come up with an example of identity markers intersecting?
3. This short essay examines class and global consumer dynamics as they relate to international women's rights activism. How are other identity categories, such as race or nationality, implicated in the above examples?

CASE STUDY EXERCISE

Think of a popular women's rights campaign. It could be one you have volunteered for, have heard about recently in the media, or one you find online through a quick search. Outline the aims of the organization and the ways in which those goals are reached. Does the organization fundraise and/ or raise awareness through selling a product? Try to trace where the products come from and examine your findings. Who is involved? For example, who physically makes the products and what demographic buys them? How does buying this product contribute to or detract from the broader aims of the organization? Most importantly, how do the product sales work towards achieving global gender equality?

REFERENCES

Bair, J. (2010). On difference and capital: Gender and the globalization of production. *Signs: Journal of Women in Culture and Society, 36*(1), 203–226.

Cho, S., Crenshaw, K., & McCall, L. (2013). Toward a field of intersectionality studies: Theory, applications, and praxis. *Signs, 38*(4), 785–810.

Daley, P. (2013). Rescuing African bodies: Celebrities, consumerism, and neoliberal humanitarianism. *Review of African Political Economy, 40*(137), 375–393.

King, S. (2004). Pink Ribbons Inc: Breast cancer activism and the politics of philanthropy. *Journal of Qualitative Studies in Education, 17*(4), 473–492.

Mahrouse, G. (2014). *Conflicted commitments: Race, privilege, and power in transnational solidarity activism.* Montreal: McGill-Queen's University Press.

Mohanty, C. (2003). Cartographies of struggle: Third world women and the politics of feminism. In C. T. *Mohanty* (Ed.), *Feminism without borders: Decolonizing theory, practicing solidarity* (pp. 43–84). Durham: Duke University Press.

Mohanty, C. (2013). Feminist encounters: Locating the politics of experience. In C. McCann & S. K. Kim (Eds.), *Feminist theory reader: Local and global perspectives* (pp. 536–552). New York, NY & London: Routledge.

Mostafanezhad, M. (2014). Volunteer tourism and the popular humanitarian gaze. *Geoforum, 54*, 111–118. doi:10.1016/j.geoforum.2014.04.004

Nomi network. (2014, February 12). Retrieved from http://www.buyherbagnotherbody.com/

Red. (2014, March 31). Retrieved from http://www.red.org/en

Richey, L., & Ponte, S. (2011). *Brand aid: Shopping well to save the world.* Minneapolis, MN: University of Minnesota Press.

Sevenly Causebox. (2015, March 24). Retrieved from http://www.sevenly.org/collections/prints

Trades of Hope. (2014a, January 13). Retrieved from http://www.tradesofhope.com/

Trades of Hope: Our Story. (2014b, January 13). Retrieved from http://www.tradesofhope.com/our-story.html

Youde, J. (2009). Ethical consumerism or reified neoliberalism? Product (RED) and private funding for public goods. *New Political Science, 31*(2), 201–220.

SARRAH J. GRUBB

10. REFLECTIONS ON RURAL

Why Place Can Be Privilege and How "Common Sense"
Understandings Hurt Rural Students

What we can see depends heavily on what our culture has trained us to look for.

(Nell Painter, 2010)

The other day, I was listening to a popular podcast that broadcasts from Los Angeles. The banter is usually humorous and lighthearted, but this day I heard something that made me engage a bit more than usual. The guest used the term, "flyover states" when discussing the "nothingness between LA and New York." "Flyover states" is how misinformed individuals flying from coast to coast describe the entire middle of the United States, or the part of the country that should only be viewed from an airplane. The host, surprised, commented that he didn't think people in Kansas would agree that "there wasn't anything" where they lived. The guest doubled down. She insisted, "Farm life is fine for those people, but it's not like anything interesting happens," and further perpetuated the media myth that, "There isn't anything between New York and LA except for Chicago".

This interaction was a perfect example of two ideas that work together in this essay: *hegemony* and *metrocentricity*. Hegemony is the dominance or control one group holds over the rest of society. It is a "way of knowing." Metrocentricity will be thoroughly explained throughout in the coming pages, but breaking the word apart gives you a quick understanding of the term. "Metro," having to do with cities, and "centricity," at the center. So, cities are at the center of the thinking.

Actually, metrocentricity encompasses the essence of hegemonic thinking that excludes rural kids and rural places from privilege. Since metrocentricity permeates our culture, this type of thinking excludes consideration of other places and spaces except in relation to an urban center. Hegemony, reinforced by media images, works to keep this dominant ideology in place. Dominant ideologies can change, but in the United States, the current

P. Leavy (Ed.), Privilege Through the Looking-Glass, 65–71.
© 2017 Sense Publishers. All rights reserved.

dominant ideology includes white, middle-class, metrocentric experiences, which according to television and movie screens, primarily includes urban experiences in LA, New York City, and Chicago. Through this lens, every aspect of the world is viewed and represented in relation to the city-centered thinking, and certain explanations begin to be generally accepted. When the media crafts representations, when they make claims about the way the world is, they become powerful ideological institutions. "These values seem commonsensical, universal, even unquestionable. That is, the media, like other ideological operators, are constantly hiding the gap between reality and their representations of it" (Grossberg & Whitney, 1998).

Since the late 19th century, representations from traveling stage shows to Penny on *The Big Bang Theory,* rurality has been portrayed as "gentle, generous, and thoroughly innocuous" (Bryan, 2013). But overall, the idea that one would choose to live in a rural area is unthinkably odd. After all, who would want to live without sidewalks, Starbucks, and pizza delivery?

There is a certain presumptuousness of what rural is among those who do not write, research, advocate, inhabit, or value rural areas. The misconception that rural areas are homogeneous place-holders between metropolitan areas damages the unique identity of rurality. (Rurality, interestingly enough, is underlined in spell check right now.) This understanding of the rural only allows rural areas to be identified by the traits of the nearest city. By extension, then, city-based thinking is better and should infiltrate all aspects of rural life.

To illustrate this idea, Steve Jacob and A. E. Luloff, rural sociologists, designed a project to map the cognitive processes of individuals considering the meaning of the term "rural." In their study, Jacob and Luloff asked participants to draw rural areas on a blank map of Pennsylvania. Most respondents "thought of rural places as those remaining after urban areas were accounted for...Those who indicated urban areas on the map were significantly more likely than other respondents to think of rural areas as homogeneous places" (Jacob & Luloff, 1995). Basically, the rural area is just a uniform placeholder between Philadelphia and Pittsburgh. Metrocentricity is so pervasive in American culture that recognizing the existence of other viable places and spaces requires intentionality.

The implications and impact for rural students is significant, especially considering that even their teachers hold popularly conceived notions of what constitutes the rural. The media impacts every part of daily life, including schooling. Students interact with media and develop their identities using the representations they view, and the adults in schools have done the same.

In spite of their own best interests, they perpetuate dominant ideological representations (Fisherkeller, 2007).

Using hegemonic thinking, rurality is part of our "history" as a country, but is far removed from the present-day. In 1897 in Iowa, a committee of twelve individuals, including the state school superintendent, completed a report commissioned by the National Educational Association on how to fix "the rural problem" (Reynolds, 1999). The result was the school consolidation movement that yoked together two or more smaller districts, pulled students out of their home schools, and disrupted communities. The Committee of Twelve pinpointed the sheer number of small rural schools as an issue. Consolidation of school districts was recommended, as they noted the "backwardness" of rural townships and school boards, and questioned abilities of the populace to sustain an "appropriate" and "modern" education for rural school children.

Consolidation as a public education policy has gained considerable steam since the late 19th century and is a popular method to achieve "efficiency," as it is assumed that a small school cannot meet the needs of its students and the costs involved in sustaining small schools are greater than the benefits. Since the consolidation movement hit full swing in the 1930s, public school districts, which once numbered around 200,000, now number close to 15,000 (Ainsbury, 2005; Tonn, 2007). The arguments for consolidation have not changed much in the last 100 years. It is a commonsense understanding that rural schools are assumed to be too costly to operate, too stupid, and too backward to keep up with modern innovation.

Even now, consolidation is a theme that State Boards of Education tend to prefer. Bigger schools are thought to be more efficient and better able to meet the needs of students, despite research that shows consolidation to be expensive [and 'almost never' ends up saving taxpayers as much as policymakers predict" (Tonn, 2007)], both in real financial amounts and community emotional cost. A district I worked in was consolidated from township schools where some students could easily walk to school, to a K-12 building where nearly all children had to be bussed. The consolidation of the high school grades happened in the late 1960s, and the middle school and elementary grades left their smaller buildings to join on one campus in the late 1990s. Until approximately 2010, alumni still met by township, instead of under the title of the local school district. There is deep emotion tied to the loss of the township schools. The preference for consolidation enforces hegemonic ideas that "bigger is better" and rural people do not know what is best for their own communities and children. The thinking is so pervasive, that when consolidation is proposed, many rural educators – with metrocentric understandings due to their own consumption of the dominant ideology – also reinforce the commonsense thinking, to their own detriment and against the wishes of their own communities.

These are possibly the same educators who view their students as less intelligent than suburban students and view their parents as not valuing education. As a teacher of gifted students in a rural school, I walked up against this belief more than once. A popular misconception was that our rural gifted students weren't gifted to the same degree as the gifted students in the well-known suburban school an hour west. Criterion for giftedness doesn't change by location, but access to resources most certainly does impact outcomes for students.

Unfortunately, "Even hometown teachers have low expectations for their [rural students'] success" (DeYoung & Lawrence, 1995). In a 2007 study of college expectations of two districts in a rural county in western Ohio, Finnie, Grubb, and McFaddin found that in grades six, nine, and twelve, approximately 90% of the students had post-secondary aspirations. What was painfully obvious, however, was that twelfth-grade students did not know the steps to take to arrive in the halls of higher learning the following fall. This gap between aspiration and achievement was due to an ignorance of process, not lack of intelligence. While inadequate guidance counseling seemed to be one culprit, none of the colleges or universities within an hour radius sponsored active recruitment efforts in the county (Finnie, Grubb, & McFaddin, 2007).

This marginalization of rural schools and students is continuous and harmful, as well as constructed under a false assumption. Many innovations in education, such as multi-age classrooms and community-based education, have originated from the rural field (Sherwood, 2000). It is hard to believe the arguments against the rural when larger, more urban districts are trying find ways to make their schools feel smaller because of the evidence that small schools "have a positive effect on student learning and well-being" (Jimerson, 2006). In one rural district where I worked, the school was leaps and bounds ahead of the more affluent, suburban districts in educational technology. With little startup capital besides the ingenuity of teachers, who used grant writing and connections to organizations casting off business equipment to acquire technology, they successfully taught students to refurbish machines and instructed faculty on best practices for utilization in the classroom. They were on the cutting edge for technology implementation in the state.

Yet, the metropolitan model of schooling is attacking the fundamental base of rural schools, which is their "connection to community" (DeYoung & Lawrence, 1995), especially when considering the arena of achievement testing. National accountability initiatives encourage states to issue mandates that require sameness, and thereby ignore differences and individualized needs. Teachers of tested areas are placed under a community microscope, as accountability testing judges their worth within the classroom and reports it directly to the public. The reporting is done at the district and building level, so individual teachers are not named. However, since there is only one teacher per grade level in small, departmentalized buildings, teachers are indirectly attached to test results. Furthermore, because schools are small and results are reported in percentages, one student can bear more than one percent of the accountability reporting. So, depending on the student groups' aptitude from year-to-year, achievement results can vary widely. Additionally, teachers in small schools are able to assess which particular students "caused" a downward fluctuation; failing to meet adequate yearly progress goals can be attached to an individual student's face (Jimerson, 2005) which may have negative implications for the student. The colorful charts from the report card are used to shame districts whose main crime is not to exist in a more populous, affluent zip code.

In the midst of this hegemonic national discussion, with suburban schools as a lens for what is normal in schools, it is easy to assume that there is nothing of worth between New York and LA but Chicago. Centering on metro areas reinforces the belief that that "bigger is better," and therefore, any school, teacher, or student who does not fit into the frame must have a deficit. This "deficit thinking" privileges the commonsense understandings of how the world works and how children and adults should behave and respond in school. If suburban schools are normal, then everything that isn't must need to be adjusted until it is functioning "correctly" by mirroring methods, functions, and beliefs of the metro-centered institution.

This metrocentricity prevents a true understanding of diversity in schools, in the sense that privileged members of society make rules, develop the language, and set the expectations for how society lives, works, and interacts. Hegemony ensures only some voices are "heard." A real appreciation for differences in histories, understandings, and experiences can only happen when privileged people realize that we are all better when we disrupt this type of thinking. Rebelling against commonsense understandings of "why things are the way they are" is important for sharing power, reversing marginalization, and acknowledging that a variety of people and places connect the spaces between New York and LA.

DISCUSSION QUESTIONS

1. What is rural to you? If you had to define rural without the help of Google, what would you say? What mental pictures accompany your definition? Does rural have a positive connotation or a negative one? Why do you think you have your understanding of rural?
2. Create a human continuum. In class or with a group of friends, line up according to the place of your high school: rural on one end, suburban in the middle, and urban at the other end. Where did the majority of your class/friends attend high school? In the context of this essay, what might the human continuum show regarding your understandings of rural?
3. Using Google, define "rural" and then "urban." What do you notice about the rural definitions that are *not* true of the urban definitions? Why might those differences be important to note?

   In the next 48 hours of your media consumption, note when and how rural is mentioned. Give examples. Are these mentions positive or negative? How so? If rural isn't mentioned at all, consider why this might be the case.

REFERENCES

Aisbury, T. L., & Shaw, N. L. (2005). Policy implications for social justice in district consolidation. *Leadership and Policy in Schools, 4*(2), 105–126.

Bryan, M. E. (2013). Yeoman and barbarians: Popular outland caricature and American identity. *Journal of Popular Culture, 46*(3), 463–480.

Campbell, A. M., & Yates, G. C. R. (2011). Want to be a country teacher? No, I am too metrocentric. *Journal of Research in Rural Education, 26*(4), 1–12.

DeYoung, A. J., & Lawrence, B. (1995). On hoosiers, Yankees, and mountaineers. *Phi Delta Kappan, 77*(2), 104–112.

Fisherkeller, J. (2007). How do kids' self-identities relate to media experiences in everyday life? In S. R. Mazzarella (Ed.), *20 Questions about youth and the media.* New York, NY: Peter Lang Publishing.

Flyover Country – TV Tropes. (n.d.). Retrieved from http://tvtropes.org/pmwiki/pmwiki.php/Main/FlyoverCountry

Grossberg, L., Wartella, E., & Whitney, D. C. (1998). *Mediamaking: Mass media in a popular culture.* Thousand Oaks, CA: Sage Publications.

Jacob, S., & Luloff, A. (1995). Exploring the meaning of rural through cognitive maps. *Rural Sociology, 60*(2), 260–276.

Jimerson, L. (2005). Placism in NCLB—how rural children are left behind. *Equity and Excellence in Education, 38*, 211–219.

Jimerson, L. (2006). *The hobbit effect: Why small works in public schools* (Rural Trust Policy Brief Series on Rural Education). Arlington, VA: The Rural Schools and Community Trust.

Painter, N. (2010). *The history of White people.* New York, NY: W.W. Norton & Company. [Kindle version]. Retrieved from Amazon.com

Reynolds, D. R. (1999). *There goes the neighborhood: Rural school consolidation at the grass roots in early twentieth-century Iowa.* Iowa City: University of Iowa Press.

Sherwood, T. (2000). Where has all the "Rural" gone? Rural education research and current federal reform. *Journal of Research in Rural Education, 16*(3), 159–167.

Tonn, J. (2007). Savings from school consolidation plans uncertain. *Education Week, 26*(29), 10.

TONY E. ADAMS

11. BEING A (GAY) DUCK IN A FAMILY OF (HETEROSEXUAL) SWANS[1]

Familial experiences of sexuality, especially lesbian, gay, bisexual, and queer (LGBQ) sexualities, often have unique characteristics – characteristics that do not resemble the experiences of other identities such as gender, age, and ethnicity. With gender, for example, families often consist of men and women; being female or male is not necessarily deviant or inherently wrong, and there is an expectation that families will be composed of cisgender men and women.[2] Some families may have more men than women, or more women than men, but family members, especially children, will often be exposed to different genders by way of sisters and brothers, grand/fathers and grand/mothers, and aunts and uncles. As such, many families understand that men and women exist, recognize that children did not choose to be male or female, and tend to not hate family members *solely* because they are female or male.[3]

Age functions similarly: Many families include multiple generations, and a child will typically learn that people have ages and aging is expected. Within some families, age and aging is sometimes celebrated, e.g., birthday parties, quinceañeras, Bar and Bat Mitzvahs, and anniversaries. As such, families tend to understand that different ages exist, recognize that children did not choose their ages, and tend to not hate family members *solely* because of age.

Ethnicity also possesses unique characteristics. Families often have one (or a few) ethnicity in common, and should two people reproduce biologically, the child will tend to share characteristics of these parents' ethnicities. Under these circumstances, I have never heard of instances of parents *not* accepting *their* child *solely* because of the child's ethnicity. Further, the child may be exposed to the same (few) ethnicities throughout much of their early life, and a family might reject a child who befriends or dates others of different ethnicities.

At an early age, a child may come to an awareness about particular genders, ages, and ethnicities, but not necessarily about sexuality, especially LGBQ experiences. Sexuality may be treated as a taboo topic, and "sexual

P. Leavy (Ed.), Privilege Through the Looking-Glass, 73–78.
© 2017 Sense Publishers. All rights reserved.

education" may be the primary, and only, context in which sexuality is ever discussed. (Could we expect a child to have courses in "gender education," "age education," or "ethnicity education?") Further, family members may share and celebrate *hetero*sexuality – that is, girls' attraction to boys and boys' attraction to girls, not necessarily a child's attraction to girls, boys, and to people who do not align with such rigid gender categories.

A child may not learn about sexuality and/or LGBQ experiences until later in life, especially if they were raised in heteronormative contexts, contexts that privilege different-sexed/gendered attraction and frame persons as heterosexual until proven otherwise (Adams, 2011). As such, an LGBQ-identified child might be the *only* LGBQ-identified person in a family; as Weston (1991) remarks, "those who come out [as LGBQ] find themselves called upon to explain how it is that a duck could have come from a family of swans" (p. 75). The LGBQ child may thus assume the sole task/burden of not only introducing sexuality as a topic of conversation but also having to explain what it means to be LGBQ. Further, the LGBQ child may encounter family members who do not accept same-sex/gender attraction or who believe that it is the child's responsibility/fault for choosing to be LGBQ, particularly if the LGBQ child is the only LGBQ person in the family or that family members have ever known.[4]

In this chapter, I describe some of my experiences with being the first, and still only, openly self-identified gay person in my family – a (gay) duck in a family of (heterosexual) swans. I describe the estrangement I felt, and continue to feel, because of my sexuality, as well as the tension and sadness that have characterized my familial experiences for more than a decade. I conclude with questions about sexuality, LGBQ identity, and family life.

***

For the first twenty years of my life (1979–1999), I lived in a rural, industrial town of approximately 25,000 people. My mother is an only child and my father has one sister, my aunt. My aunt and her husband, my uncle, have one child, my cousin, who is ten years older than me. Although I have a biological half-sister, I was raised as an only child. I have a few distant cousins, but I consider my mother, father, aunt, uncle, and cousin my primary family members.

I was the first person in my family to identify as gay. I told my mother – that is, "came out" to her as gay – in 2001. In 2003, one month after my paternal grandmother's death, I told my father, aunt, uncle, and cousin.

I did not receive much support from them after coming out. At best, I received lukewarm comments such as, "I think you're too young to know if you are gay" and "I once knew a gay man; he was okay." My dad refused to speak to me for six months, and my aunt did not allow me to visit her for a few years; she did not want a gay person in her house.

"At least your parents didn't physically harm or disown you," I heard from some of my friends, comments which suggested I should appreciate my family's lukewarm responses, stay quiet and feel lucky, and recognize that other LGBQ children have it much worse than me. Although I recognize that others may experience terrible consequences after coming out, I also cannot dismiss the pain of my family's responses; their lack of support never felt good.

***

To be fair to my family, and to better understand their lack of support, I need to describe the repressive, heterosexual contexts in which I was raised, and contexts to which I too contributed. Family members frequently discussed and celebrated heterosexuality, particularly men being sexually attracted to women and women being sexually attracted to men. Both of my parents have been (heterosexually) married multiple times, and before I came out, I had been to numerous female strip clubs with my father. My cousin once referred to me as "the family faggot" and would tease me about being attracted to men; he even hired one of his female friends, a sex worker, to come to my father's house to (try to) have sex with me. I had a friend who wanted to have a celebration for me when I lost my virginity (with a woman), and people regularly asked me about my sexual experiences with women (but not about my sexual experiences with men).

Given such heterosexual pressure, I often said that I wanted to be a priest, a stated desire which quelled suspicions and questions about my sexuality. When it became obvious that I wouldn't pursue the priesthood, I tried to have three serious, yet erratic, relationships with women, each of which lasted about six months. I was also aggressively homophobic; I didn't want others to suspect my sexuality and so I ridiculed gay men and lesbians as much as possible. These contexts illustrate why coming out was not only difficult for me, but also why it fractured many of my familial relationships.

***

As I mentioned, my aunt did not allow me to visit her after I came out as gay. A few years after her refusal, I spent a week with her in a hospital where my father underwent surgery for colon cancer. During our time together, she told me stories about family members, particularly her parents and brother (my dad), never approving of Jake, her husband (my uncle), and how she had to disregard their beliefs in order to marry him.

"Isn't it curious that family members may not approve of the people we love?" I said. "Others didn't approve of Jake for various reasons. Family members don't approve of my partner because he is male and because I am male. Like you, I frequently have to disregard others' beliefs and defend the person I love."

"It is curious," she replied and said nothing more. I did not ask if she felt bad for refusing to allow me to visit or waiting six years to meet my (male) partner.

***

In my book, *Narrating the Closet* (Adams, 2011), I described the ways in which my relationships were harmed because of my sexuality. I mentioned how my aunt did not allow me to visit, but in order to protect her privacy, I disguised my aunt as a "cousin."

In 2014, immediately after reading this section of the book, my father called me.

"Which cousin wouldn't allow you to visit?" he asked.

"It wasn't a cousin," I replied, "it was your sister [my aunt]."

"She wouldn't allow you to visit?" he asked. "Why didn't you tell me?"

"Dad," I said, "we didn't have the best relationship when it happened, and we did not talk about my sexuality. I especially felt uncomfortable reprimanding your sister."

"Don't live your life for her," he replied. "You have a great life and I am proud of you."

His comments indicate an evolved support for me and suggest that I should disregard his sister's actions – a suggestion that further estranges me from her and possibly estranges her from him. Although his comment indicates the slow progress he and I have made in our relationship, it also demonstrates the ways in which my sexuality continues to fracture familial bonds.

***

After the June 2015 United States Supreme Court ruling in support of same-sex/gender marriage, I assumed that I would experience supportive responses about the ruling from family members. However, both of my parents only commented neutrally about the case, and neither asked if I will marry my partner of seven years – an avoidance that, at least to me, still indicates silence regarding my sexuality. Further, when I posted praise for the ruling on Facebook, an online context in which my mother, father, and aunt participate, none of them "liked" the post – another silence that stands in stark contrast to the many other posts of mine that they like.

***

At a cousin's wedding, an event that took place two weeks after the Supreme Court ruling, a wedding I avoided because I assumed that talk about, and praise of, heterosexuality would be present, my mother reported that the minister aggressively insisted that marriage should be reserved only for a woman and a man. My mother was upset by the message, immediately relayed it back to me, and said that I made a good decision to not attend.

I am saddened to realize that more than a decade after I came out, I still find myself not only avoiding a family event, but also one which celebrated heterosexuality and (supposedly) dismissed the possibility of same-sex/gender marriage. I am saddened to realize that, in order to protect myself from uneasy silences and disparaging discourse, I must refrain from fully participating in family life and continue to live as a duck among swans.

DISCUSSION QUESTIONS

1. I opened this chapter by describing potential differences between familial experiences of gender, age, and ethnicity and experiences of sexuality. Do you agree with these differences? Why (not)? In what ways may familial experiences of gender, age, and ethnicity be similar to experiences of sexuality? When did you first learn about gender, age, ethnicity, and sexuality?
2. What advice do you have for people who are the only LGBQ-identified people in their family? How should they educate heterosexual family members about LGBQ experiences? How long should LGBQ-identified persons tolerate familial ignorance and prejudice toward their sexuality?
3. Do families need to approve of those their children date or marry? How long are family members able to disapprove of a relationship? One year? Ten years? What if such disapproval never disappears, or only exists because of another person's gender, age, ethnicity, and/or sexuality?

NOTES

[1] I borrow the duck-swan metaphor from Weston's (1991) comments about how a person who identifies as lesbian, gay, bisexual, and/or queer might feel living among heterosexual family members and in contexts that celebrate heterosexuality (p. 75).

[2] I recognize that some families and cultures value cisgender men and women differently. I only want to stress that families often consist of men and women; biological, all-male and all-female families are difficult to sustain.

[3] These assumptions perpetuate the male-female gender binary and primarily apply to cisgender family members; they do not represent the experiences of families and family members who identify as genderqueer, transgender, or intersexed (Dreger & Herndon, 2009; Norwood & Lannutti, 2015).

[4] Some families have multiple LGBQ-identified persons. However, I assume that many families do not have an abundance of LGBQ-identified persons, at least when compared to family members who identify as heterosexual.

REFERENCES

Adams, T. E. (2011). *Narrating the closet: An autoethnography of same-sex attraction.* Walnut Creek, CA: Left Coast Press.

Dreger, A. D., & Herndon, A. M. (2009). Progress and politics in the intersex rights movement. *GLQ, 15*, 199–224.

Norwood, K. M., & Lannutti, P. J. (2015). Families' experiences with transgender identity and transition: A family stress perspective. In L. G. Spencer & J. C. Capuzza (Eds.), *Transgender communication studies: Histories, trends, and trajectories* (pp. 51–68). Lanham, MD: Lexington.

Weston, K. (1991). *Families we choose: Lesbians, gays, kinship.* New York, NY: Columbia University Press.

TAMMY BIRD

12. SWIRLING SHADES OF RIGHT AND WRONG

1984

We were sitting side-by-side on her porch swing, our feet moving heel-to-toe, heel-to-toe, heel-to-toe in comfortable unison. Our children, seven months apart in their third year, quietly stacked interconnecting reds and blues and greens higher and higher against the white-washed porch. We spent many hours here, the four of us, our husbands away at work, our nearest neighbors a quarter mile in the distance.

"My sis's coming".

Four words; well, three in her southern speak. It took me almost my whole first year to get used to the way people in the South run words together. We don't do that in Colorado.

Toni was younger than my neighbor by two years and separated in thought and actions by an entire continuum. I met her once, the year before.

I picked up my sweet tea glass and laid the rim against my lip. The cool liquid felt good against my tongue. I swallowed. "When?"

I wanted to say more, but it suddenly felt very crowded in my mouth, and very hot inside my belly. I hoped she couldn't tell. I tried to breathe deep, to send the cool air of the early summer day down to my gut where colors and textures were running together until they could never be pulled apart into what they had been.

Toni. Her name entered with the last deep breath. I closed my mouth, looked at my daughter playing in front of me, and waited until it was safe to exhale.

"Will ya be here? Could use the support." My neighbor's southern drawl almost faded away in the softness of her request.

I watched a drip of condensation move from the bottom of the tall, thick glass in my hand to the tanned skin right above my knee.

"Hey," she added, obviously sensing something in my silence. "I get it if'n you ain't up for it. Hell. I ain't myself".

P. Leavy (Ed.), Privilege Through the Looking-Glass, 79–84.

I shook my head. "Oh, Charlotte, no. Of course I will be here. No worries. Just give me a time." I never told her what had happened the year before, and I knew I never would.

Our feet started moving again, slightly out of sync. I adjusted my timing to bring my end of the swing back into harmony with hers.

"Two'clock, or there 'bouts. Kinda glad ta see 'er. Just...ya know. Wish she'd find 'erself a nice man".

I nodded slowly, my head following the rhythm of her words and the movement of our feet.

We were quiet for a long time. The sway of the swing and the slight squeak between the wood and the eye-bolt that allowed the chains their perpetual back and forth movement brought the porch scene back into balance.

I thought about what it meant to have Toni back in our little town. She was different from anyone I had ever met.

That first day, the first day I met Toni, I watched her wrestle with the kids in the yard. She easily scooped a kid up under each arm and spun around and around until the three of them fell giggling into the grass. "Why is she so muscular?" I whispered across the kitchen to Charlotte when we went in to dish up the peach pecan cobbler that had been cooling on the stove. "She kinda looks like a guy".

"She ain't a guy 'cause she has muscles".

"I know, but..." I let my voice trail off. It was just weird. The male-cut t-shirt tucked into belted Levi's that sat low on her hips, and the hair as short as my little brother's standing straight up on her head. The way she swung her cowboy boot up to her knee and slouched down in the porch chair. The way she didn't move to help us in the kitchen, but stayed on the porch with my husband and Charlotte's husband.

Later on that first day, she asked me if I wanted to go into town with her, said she needed some women stuff. Now I wondered if she used that excuse so the men wouldn't offer to come along. They didn't.

***

Weirdly, having sex with Toni didn't feel wrong. If I had been single. If I hadn't had a family. If I was a man. But I wasn't any of those things. I also wasn't someone who thought sex outside of marriage was okay. Married is married, and hurting my husband felt awful.

The day after Toni left, I told him.

"I had sex with Toni."

His face lost its square. "You? When?"

"It was just a thing. You know. I still love you, and I am still with you…"

I wanted to keep talking, to fill the space with words, but the space refused to be filled.

It was more than just a thing.

I knew that, standing there watching the masculine square fall out of his face.

I knew that, standing there remembering the disorienting pleasure that was Toni.

I knew that, standing there with the man who had promised to love, honor, and protect.

For me, our love had a plastic, glossy feel to it, but it was safe and normal. I wasn't sure, but I didn't think it was like that for him. I wondered why it was like that for me. I wondered, but not enough to let myself out of the mold that I knew I was supposed to live in. I'd heard of lesbians, suspected Toni was one that first day when I watched her muscles ripple throughout her body as she played with the kids on the lawn. I wasn't that. I was soft and girly. I loved to put on a dress and makeup for a night on the town. I loved the feel of my hair against my back when I wore a spaghetti-strap top.

Yet I wanted to see her again, to hold her like I had in the back of Charlotte's car. I wanted her to keep looking at me the way she had when she was between my legs in the dark of the cramped backseat, all keen attention and wonder.

Everything jumbled together in my head like broken glass.

I looked at my husband, thought about our children. If I could figure it out, would it matter? I looked around the room. The happy family picture stared at me from the dresser. We wore matching blues and yellows. Smiles that said, "We are a happy little unit." Our bed. The quilt from Cracker Barrel. It had patchwork squares that reminded us both of our grandmothers. I lowered my fingers to the part I could reach. The little bumps of fabric between the lines of thread reminding me where I came from. I was a wife and mother. The symbolism of that fact felt rough under the skin of my fingertips.

"You had sex with her." His voice sounded far away from our bedroom. "In a car".

"But I love you." I didn't look at him when I said it. I looked at the family on the dresser. My tears blurred the blue and yellow, swirling the soft shades into a pool of unrecognizable ripples. I tried to reshape the image by blinking quickly, by pulling my eyelids up and my cheekbones down.

"So. What now?" His words were matter-of-fact. Like him. Just like that, he had absorbed the gut punch and re-squared his jaw. "Sounds like you have shit to figure out. Do not think for one minute, though, that you will pull the children into your disgusting little game".

Bam. His punch. Harder than any I could throw.

My decision was made. My place was here, and there was no room for childish games. Later, alone in the bathroom, I crumpled the paper that held her number, threw it in the toilet, and flushed.

From time to time I remembered Toni looking up at me, her body curved to fit between the door and the maroon leather of the back seat, her t-shirt hanging on one shoulder, exposing the pale white of her flesh. The dark luminous image of her eyes on my own tanned nakedness, as they used the fissures in my skin to push through the dullness inside me. The way she studied my face with complete attention. The way the streetlight's glow from hundreds of yards away somehow made its way through a cracked window and onto the small rose-colored nipples that sat barely higher than her skin. I remembered. I remembered affection, and embarrassment, and lust, and shame.

Three hundred and sixty-five days passed with gatherings of friends and families, with first teeth and first steps, with obligatory sex and thoughts of a woman I couldn't want and couldn't have. I spent more time hating myself than I had before I met her, before I let myself experiment.

Experiment. That is what he called it. He being my husband. I let him. And I let myself believe him. We built an image of me for us, for everyone: the dutiful, wonderful wife and mother who loved flowers on the table and supper on the stove. Three hundred and sixty-five days passed watching Disney movies cuddled on the couch as a family.

But it wasn't the same. I was gray inside.

Toni returned on day 366. Exactly one year and one day after I knew I liked sex with girls, one girl, anyway. Exactly one year and one day after I told him and he told me it was a phase to get through. Exactly one year and one day after I decided that I hate flowers on the table and supper on the stove, at least in this house, with this person. None of that knowing changed anything for me in the 1980's.

Toni looked the same, and when I hugged her she smelled the same – like peach deodorant and lemon shampoo. All citrusy and sweet. I wanted to kiss her. I went to bed every night that week knowing that she was next door and I was here, lying next to my husband, in the bed where our children were conceived. It was almost a relief when she turned to wave at us from the top step of the bus. Whatever Toni and I were, maybe it wasn't a thing you could fit into a jar. Maybe it needed a wide-open space or an entirely new universe.

Whatever we were, I was glad she was leaving. I was glad that I wouldn't have to deal with the numbness I felt at home knowing she was next door.

We didn't touch during her second visit, unless you count the hug hello and hug goodbye. In fact, it would be many years before I would allow myself to explore who I was, who she had unleashed. I had an obligation to my husband, my children, my friends, my neighborhood, and society, and I played my role well, but I never stopped knowing that regardless of what society said I had to be, whatever had been between us in those brief moments felt different, deep, fathomless.

2017

Toni taught me in one night what it meant to be a woman in the 1980's. Prior to that night, I thought everyone was the same at their core, that if you were a woman, or you were a man, that is what you were, as defined by society. It was okay to feel numb inside as long as you followed the path created for you from the moment the pink or blue blanket was wrapped tight around your wiggling form. Today, so many more of us understand that the space between right and wrong is so small, if there is a space at all. So many understand that terms such as men and women and gay and straight, are restrictive and limiting. The LGB community has become the LGBTQIA community, and growing.

I had a professor once, years after Toni woke my body to what could be, who spoke of continuums and disjunctive bars. I sat in her class and imagined that bar spinning, the momentum sometimes moving it left and sometimes right.

Life is like that. The spinning. The continuum. For years, we have gained momentum in the movement for equality. For years, the continuum pendulum has moved life in the direction of inclusion. My children are now grown. I am now married to a wonderful woman whose story of coming out, or not, is much like mine. Most days I feel safe, surrounded by family and friends who love us exactly where we are on the continuum. However, in the year 2017, 33 years after I experienced *Me* for the first time, there are still 27 states where you can be fired for your sexual orientation or your gender identity. There are still 28 states where you can be evicted or denied housing for your sexual orientation or gender identity. Stop and let that soak in for a moment. People have asked why women and men all over the world came together on January 21, 2017. The reasons are as varied as the women and men who came together in solidarity. For me, the reason was clear. I never want a little girl to keep her hair long for fear of being called a boy, or a young mom to stay in a marriage for fear she will lose her children if she leaves, or a boy to be forced to wear girl's clothing by his parents because he was born with a vagina.

Today, as people around the world march for the rights of women and the freedom for all, I am reminded that among the many things we march for, we march to remind our sisters and those who love us that the battle for LGBTQIA equality cannot end.

DISCUSSION QUESTIONS

1. How have custody laws changed between 1984 and 2017? Would this woman face discrimination in court today? Defend your response using court cases and research.
2. Reflect on your own gender and sexual positioning within the current culture. Discuss a time when you have experienced discrimination, or have witnessed those in positions other than your own face discrimination.
3. After reading this chapter, read *The Story of X* by Lois Gould. Analyze what the two authors are saying about society and cultural norms as it pertains to gender and sexuality.

EM RADEMAKER

13. MALE OR FEMALE?

Everyday Life When the 'Or' Is 'And'

Note: I feel it would be a disservice to the intention of this essay and indeed this book, if I did not recognize that my experience in gender is my own. I aim to help you as the reader see how gender can be experienced in ways different to what is taught broadly. I do not wish to claim the nonbinary experience as being singular to my own (you will hopefully see the irony in this later), nor belittle the privilege that I have within the nonbinary experience.

There is nothing particularly extraordinary about me. I love dogs and grew up reading Harry Potter. I have tattoos and I listen to Johnny Cash. I've got acne scars, and if I'm being honest with myself, am a bit overweight. I think you would find me to be an average young American, as would I. When most people look at me, they see a tall, Caucasian female who wears a lot of black. This observation is technically correct, but incomplete. I'm not female… sometimes. I identify outside of the traditional gender binary.

What is that? A gender binary? Well, as humans, we categorize everything. It's one of the first things we do as babies. Is this safe or unsafe? Can I eat that or not? Do I like this color or prefer that color? We have created two prominent categories to differentiate between biological parts. Woman equals breasts and vagina. Man equals penis. Early in our societal history, we began to add roles to the other side of the equal sign. Woman now also equals mother, sister, aunt, and daughter. Man equals father, brother, uncle, and son. Eventually, we began to attribute characteristics, behaviors, and responsibilities. Woman equals beautiful, submissive, and child-rearing. Man equals strong, dominant, and protector.

The categories expanded from defining physical features to claiming certain actions and experiences for one group of people over another. There is a clear and reasonable explanation as to why this happened, but I recommend taking an introductory anthropology course for that. The footnotes version is this: our society has constructed ideas of male and female and what it means

P. Leavy (Ed.), Privilege Through the Looking-Glass, 85–93.

to identify as such. However, we have not constructed at all, or at most, as well, what it means to identify not as female and not as male, but as a gender beyond.

I think it is best to get some personal details out of the way early. In the gender identity category (my personally constructed idea of what it means to be female and what it means to be male), my "femaleness" and my "maleness" fluctuate every day. Some days both are high, and on others, both are low or nonexistent. On others, it is more pronounced as one over the other. I have no control over this fluctuation and it can happen at any time.

In the gender expression box (how I present my gender identity through physical appearance, actions, voice, etc.), I also fluctuate. I tend to wear the color black and somewhat universally gender-appropriated clothing (jeans, t-shirts, blazers, and so forth). This helps me to feel more in control if my gender should shift unexpectedly, because I do not look overtly masculine or feminine. I do often rock a bold red lip though, as makeup gives me power regardless of how I identify.

In regard to biological sex, I am 100% female, though due to a condition called polycystic ovarian syndrome (PCOS), my hormones are imbalanced. Some people could cite an excess of testosterone as a bit of male-ness; I do not.

In regard to sexual attraction and romantic attraction, I have the possibility of being attracted to anyone regardless of gender, sex, or expression. This does not mean that I am attracted to everyone, rather that someone's gender, expression, or sex is not the primary factor that induces attraction. For me, a person's intelligence and character are the prioritized factors.

In summary, my gender is fluid. Some days it presents as feminine, others as masculine, sometimes as both, and occasionally as neither. For people like myself, the lack of context for how to present oneself as outside of the gender binary creates challenges to overcome, some of which you may be aware and some which never would have crossed your mind. Allow me to lead you through a few examples:

I'm not a morning person, so waking up is already a less than enjoyable task. Still, most days my commitment to my job motivates my feet to trod off to the shower and I am able to emerge a more pleasant person within five to ten minutes. I find it's vital to start the day with a mood booster as I'm guaranteed to confront several disheartening choices throughout the day.

And so, we come to the first challenge: how do I want to look today? Everyone must answer this question at some point, and like everyone, I calculate the expected influencing factors:

1. Where am I headed? Is it formal or informal? *We'll say that today I am going to work. My office is a business-casual environment with noted emphasis on the casual. (It is not unusual to see cargo pants and Hawaiian shirts)*
2. What is the weather like? *I live in Juneau, AK, so more often than not, I need to adapt to the rain.*
3. Who will I see? *While I typically interact with the same 10–15 people, the group consists of coworkers, staff, and my supervisor.*
   Simple questions with simple answers. For me, there is always one additional factor which I must consider:
4. How can I make my appearance reflect the gender I am, remembering that I physically have the shape most associated with a woman (breasts and curving hips)? *Today I feel more masculine than I did the day before. I would feel most comfortable if my appearance reflected my masculinity because that's how my gender is presenting.*
   a. Should I wear makeup? *It gives me confidence, but makeup is not traditionally associated with masculinity.*
   b. How should I wear my hair? *I keep my hair about shoulder length because it has versatility, but some people see long hair as a feminine feature.*
   c. Should I bind? *My breasts are a part of my body but they certainly aren't masculine, so should I try to hide them?*
   d. If I dress as a male, will my coworkers be confused? *Yesterday I wore a skirt and heels because that's what best expressed my gender.*
   e. If I present as male and have to use the restroom, which one should I visit? *My coworkers saw me use the women's restroom yesterday. Should I use the men's today? Will I make people feel uncomfortable? Will they get mad at me or complain to my boss?*

Complicated questions with complicated answers. Or no answers. Or fluid answers. Sound familiar?

Do you see how easily these simple everyday encounters can become stressful burdens for a nonbinary person? Perhaps the most difficult part to overcome is that there is no precedent or expectation for nonbinary people. If I want to emulate someone who defies gender barriers and gender norms, I can only think of a few celebrity names. While I do believe we should all aspire to be more like Ruby Rose, it's not exactly a realistic expectation for most.

***

When I leave my house, I breathe in the fresh, wild air and look for the mountain tops if the sky is clear enough. If it is summer, I may pluck a few wild blueberries and salmonberries from the nearby bushes as I make my way to my office, which is a short 100-foot walk from my front door. I greet the students who staff our administrative desk and we usually share stories from our adventures the evening before, perhaps discuss the latest episode of a mutually beloved TV show, and then I make my way to my desk. I'll work at my computer for an hour or two before heading to my first meeting of the day.

Here, I will be confronted with my second challenge. At the meeting is a new employee. I'll walk into the conference room and sit down next to the new face. It's a novelty to interact with fresh minds and I'm excited to have the new person join the team. We introduce ourselves and as usual, they have a difficult time grasping my name.

"Sorry, did you say Emma?"

"No, actually, it's just Em. The letter E and the letter M."

"Oh, is that short for something?"

"No, actually, it's just Em."

"Right, but what's on your birth certificate? Emily? Emilia?"

"No, actually, it's just Em."

"Oh, that's an unusual name."

"Thanks."

That's a near verbatim conversation that I've had at least twenty times in the past three years. I used to have a conversation that looked more like this:

"Sorry, did you say Emma?"

"No, actually, it's just Em. The letter E and the letter M."

"Oh, is that short for something?"

"No, actually, it's just Em."

"Right, but what's on your birth certificate? Emily? Emilia?"

"Well, legally my name is still Emily, because though I've started the name change process several times, it is quite an expensive and bureaucratic process."

"Oh, so why are you changing it?"

"I prefer a name that is gender-neutral because I don't identify within the gender binary. Emily was so associated with femininity that it made me uncomfortable. Many close friends and family have called me Em since I was a kid so it seemed like the logical choice".

"Oh."

Not exactly a welcoming or casual conversation when you are first getting to know someone.

Names are important, as they are, in many instances, the first identity we have. I'm happy to share my name with others and even more happy when they accept that the name I give them is the name I wish to be called. In both conversations, I felt the need to justify why my name is "different." Though I would argue that in an era where parents are naming their children after fruit and hipster trends, "Em" is hardly revolutionary.

The new employee, let's call him Mark, and I are saved from an awkward end to our conversation with the introduction of another one of our coworkers. During the meeting, we discuss various tasks we have completed or begun, and occasionally one of the veteran members of the team will fill in the details for Mark. If I am referenced, my coworkers use my preferred pronouns of they, them, and their. Mark's face shows his obvious confusion, but he doesn't call attention. After the meeting is adjourned, Mark asks me why our coworkers were using those pronouns.

"Because I prefer gender neutral pronouns."

"..."

"I identify as genderfluid."

"..."

"..."

"Oh, so you're transgender. Are you making the switch?"

"...No...I'm not making a switch to anything. I just sometimes will present more masculine and sometimes will present more feminine, depending on how my gender fluctuates. Thus, I'm more comfortable being referred to in a gender non-specific manner, and our language allows for that".

"Oh, that's cool."

"Yeah. Thanks."

Ideally, our conversation would have ended after my first statement. That's all Mark needs to know. This is my preference when people are referring to me. Unfortunately, Mark's ignorance, as blissful as it may seem, put me in the awkward position of having to "out" myself to a new acquaintance. His assertion that my preference was "cool" was an attempt to let me know that he was cool with whatever it is I was talking about, but gender isn't really all that cool. Sometimes it actually kind of sucks to be in a minority demographic. I'll let you chew on that.

In the afternoon, I have an appointment at the eye doctor and prepare myself for a third challenge. I've just switched to a new doctor because I want to discuss the possibility of Lasik surgery. As I'm filling out the intake papers, I stumble upon the options, "M/F?" I know what it means: male or female? And I know what I'm supposed to do: I'm supposed to circle one. It would be easier if they asked "M/W?" because then I would know to circle my biological sex. Male and female refer to gender. I wish there was a T for trans, but then again, why do they need to know anyway? My eye doctor won't be dealing with anything in that neck of the woods. I settle for messily circling half of M and half of F. Technically, it is the most accurate answer I could give. They can figure it out if they want.

Forms are difficult for nonbinary persons, as it is not yet commonplace to include a third option. It is either "Man or Woman" or "Female or Male." Aside from that unfortunate bypass, many forms ask for gender when they really mean sex, or they ask for sex or gender when they have no business knowing it in the first place. Personally, I don't see the point in putting sex on a driver's license. Is the picture not a more accurate (and polite) means of corroborating a person's identity? In an ideal world, there would be a write-in option for sex and a write-in option for gender. For the love of all that is equitable, let people self-identify! That would make a great bumper sticker.

At the end of the day, I walk back home, let the dog outside, and start to make dinner. I will sometimes call my family in the evenings, which is when my fourth challenge is presented. My parents live in Texas with one of my older brothers, my grandma, and some aunts, uncles, and cousins. My two other brothers live in Illinois, along with some more aunts, uncles, and cousins. I like hearing about their days and sharing stories. While they all know about my identity and are supportive, language presents the biggest challenge in feeling completely comfortable all the time. My parents have four children and I am often referred to as their only daughter. Some days this is accurate, but what other word is there to use, as I am not always a son either. My three brothers often refer to me as a sister. Some days this is accurate, but what other word is there to use, as I am not always a brother. My eldest brother is a parent to four children, and I am often referred to as Auntie Em. Some days this is accurate, but what other word is there to use, as I am not always an uncle (nor do I live in Kansas).

I like words; I majored in several languages as an undergraduate. Words help us relate and connect our thoughts to others. Finding the perfect word is one of the most truly satiating experiences I can ascertain. I have learned, however, that just because a language doesn't have a specific word for an experience or idea, does not mean that speakers of this language cannot comprehend this experience or idea. I use this knowledge when asked about my gender identity. Not everyone understands what "genderfluid" or "genderqueer" means, so I find other ways to use the individual's personal level of understanding to relay my meaning. I ask my mom and dad to call me their child. I ask my nephews and niece to call me Em. It's not an entirely equitable switch, but it'll do for the time being.

There are other matters in which my gender and gender expression become difficult to navigate, such as dating and sex. As these are intertwined with sexuality and the intersectionality can be difficult to understand, I will not explore them except to note one point of interest. As a pansexual, gender fluid individual, I have experienced attraction to a woman while feeling myself masculine, feminine, and everywhere else on the spectrum. I have experienced attraction to a man while feeling myself masculine, feminine, and everywhere else on the spectrum. I have also experienced attraction to persons not identifying as either man or woman while feeling myself masculine, feminine, and everywhere else on the spectrum. The experiences are vastly different, even though attraction is attraction. Put more simply: attraction to a woman as a woman/femme/female and attraction to a woman as a man/butch/masculine are two deeply unique feelings.

Though I am faced with certain challenges that others are not, I should also note that as a non-binary person, I have certain privileges that other non-binary and trans persons do not. It's important for me to recognize this. For example, I live very close to my work. If I were uncomfortable with my choices for using the restroom, I could walk back to my house. I also work in a reasonably open environment. I am out to my coworkers, my boss, and my staff. I am also out to my parents and family and have a strong support network. I come from a middle-class family and I am Caucasian. Each demographic has incredible privilege associated with it. Despite all of my privilege, I struggle with anxiety and depression, largely influenced by my struggle to situate my gender identity. I'm also a survivor of a suicide attempt, and I am grateful every day to still be here.

At the end of each day, I'm still me. I'm still Em. Though our society is structured with cisgender people in mind, it is not inoperable simply because I am not cisgender. I live to the fullest and am generally satisfied with my life. I am optimistic that eventually cisgender, trans, and nonbinary folk will be able to coexist equitably. For now, those people who do not have the additional burdens (nor the joys, for I do love who I am) of living as a genderfluid or genderqueer person, I ask only for your patience and recognition of the privileges that your identity allows you.

DISCUSSION QUESTIONS

1. What does it mean to be masculine? What does it mean to be a man? Is there a difference?
2. What does it mean to be feminine? What does it mean to be a woman? Is there a difference?
3. What does it mean to be androgynous? What does it mean to be intersex? Is there a difference?
4. How is gender viewed differently in cultures other than your own?
5. List all parts of your identity. Include as many demographics as you can think of.
   a. For which identities are you the majority? A minority?
   b. Which part of your identity do you prioritize? Which do you think about the most? Which has the most influence on your daily life? If there are more than one, think about how these identities intersect with each other.
   c. Imagine that you move to a new country. You now live in a culture that is very similar to your own, but there is no one who shares your highest prioritized identity (identities). How might your experiences living in this new country be different from your experiences living in previous countries?

SUGGESTED RESOURCES

The GenderBread Person: This tool has been a standard addition to many trainings I have developed and facilitated because it helps people visualize distinct but related terminology. Though the origins of the GenderBread person are controversial, I appreciate the imagery as a tool for teaching. It is available at http://itspronouncedmetrosexual.com

Move Into the Circle activity: This is one of my favorite activities when I teach privilege, identity, and intersectionality to my staff, and I'm sure there is a more creative name somewhere. The facilitator reads a statement, such as, "Move into the circle if your parents graduated from a college or university," or, "Move into the circle if you identify as a Democrat." The group recognizes these individuals and reflects on what that might mean, then the individual will step back to rejoin the group. If there is ever a statement where no one steps in, we reflect on the types of people who are not represented in our group. It can be a very stimulating and emotional activity, as it can include statements regarding challenges or hardships.

https://www.genderspectrum.org/
http://nonbinary.org/

http://genderqueerid.com/
https://www.pflag.org/
I Know Very Well How I Got My Name by Elliott DeLine.
Nothing is Right by Michael Scott Monje Jr.
Here, We Cross: a collection of queer and genderfluid poetry from Stone Telling ed. Rose Lemberg.

SHALEN LOWELL

14. TRANSCENDING GENDER BINARIZATION

The Systematic Policing of Genderfluid Identity and Presentation

My gender used to be an aspect of my person about which I never questioned; my confidence in my gender identity was unshakeable. Only until I lived abroad for a year – thrust into a new-to-me culture and a country in which I could explore myself – did I realize I no longer identified as a girl, nor as a woman, or as "female." Yet the execution of that realization, that I was transgender, did not come to full fruition until years later. In the intervening time, my life was seeded with insecurity, severe body dysphoria, and incomprehension (that's not to say I do not still experience these pressures). Only two years ago did I fully begin to accept myself as gender nonconforming, so in some senses I put off my "coming out." Returning from abroad and re-entering the conservative, religious environment in which I spent my time at college, I subconsciously tucked my gender questioning away. This was in large part due to my relative comfort in presenting how I always used to present, pretending my gender was what it used to be. Addressing my gender instilled in me more discomfort than acknowledging the realization that I am transgender and genderfluid, a harmful perpetuation of denial instilled in me from internalized, cultural transphobia. Almost for the sake of sparing myself potential ridicule from others, I rejected my identity. The overwhelming pressure of conformity, of reinforced binary presentation, damaged me for so long.

Genderfluidity is a nonbinary, non-static, gender nonconforming identity which signifies that an individual's gender is fluid, meaning that genderfluid people may identify as multiple genders at once, fluctuate between a few specific genders, or at times experience gender then no gender at all. Each individual's definition of their own genderfluidity varies as much as gender does. I use the term "genderfluid" as my gender marker, as well as an umbrella term comprising the multiple genders with which I identify (the term can be used either as a catch-all term, such as "genderqueer," or as an identity in itself). My impression remains that gender conforming individuals seek to

P. Leavy (Ed.), Privilege Through the Looking-Glass, 95–102.

constantly dissect my identity into strict binaries. However, genderfluidity is not a mere composite of gendered categories. In fact, my genderfluidity consists of several *non*binary gender identities – agender, nonbinary transguy, and general nonbinary. To me, those markers signify identities unique unto myself and my expression: when I'm agender, I identify as genderless; when nonbinary transguy, I identify as a guy, but not as a binary transguy nor a binary man; when nonbinary, I feel a vague gender that wavers here nor there, just nonbinary. Because I identify as each of these gender markers, I identify as genderfluid.

Regarding the presentation of someone who identifies as genderfluid, an ideology that's increasingly evident to me, is the reinforcement of the binary genders and gender presentations on these individuals that many genderfluid individuals seek to subvert or escape. Whether a MOGAI (marginalized orientations, gender alignments, and intersex) identifying individual or not, people who are not genderfluid continue to enforce and perpetuate a visual binary that they constitute, to which genderfluid people should adhere, in an attempt to understand their gender(s) as fluid. This perpetuation includes circulating typical presentations of hegemonic masculinity and femininity, dictating that even individuals who are gender nonconforming, such as myself, should nonetheless conform to normative standards of gender appearance, i.e. how certain genders should look and present.

For example, there is a heavy emphasis on genderfluid individuals presenting as either dichotomized masculine or feminine (for those who believe that clothing is gendered as such), and that one must have "girl days," "boy days," "feminine days," "masculine days," and the alike, each presentation is itself mutually exclusive and presentation normative. First, there is always a punctuated emphasis on the *or*, never the *and*, when binarizing genderfluid identities. You are expected to present as one gender identity/presentation *or* the other – never both, or many, simultaneously (indeed *never* any two genders or identities simultaneously) – even if you happen to identify as more than two genders. This reinforcement manifests in a polarization of identity, perhaps in an attempt for those who do not identify as genderfluid to grasp what being genderfluid signifies. Moreover, if you're like myself and identify outside the gender binary, an expectation is imposed upon you to present as the "default neutral," which is masculine. Why masculine is the expected default presentation for genderfluid individuals is beyond me. Indeed, why is "typical" masculine clothing the default style for androgyny? Are you genderfluid? If yes, then your presentation is automatically genderfluid by nature of our self-expression and self-identification. There is no *one* type of genderfluid body, and thus no *one* type of genderfluid presentation; presentation is as diverse as the number of people who are genderfluid.

Still, these stereotypical presentation norms continue to police expression. My clothing style tends to read as fairly androgynous, however I wear clothing across the whole spectrum of body presentation. While I bind with a chest binder, frequently don long- and short-sleeve button-ups, and tend not to reveal my chest, I also wear dresses, skirts, and other clothing people may describe as "female" or "feminine." However, I read all clothing as gender-neutral, in that I believe all types and styles of clothes can be worn of all genders. I do not allow the binaries placed on clothing to inhibit my gender expression. I feel most comfortable identifying outside the confines of the gender binary. Some genderfluid individuals, especially if they are bigender or trigender, do identify with binary identities and feel comfortable presenting themselves within these binaries. But polarized, binary gender identity is not integral to, nor a necessary component of, identifying as genderfluid.

Moreover, what's especially alarming to me is that these binaries are further perpetuated within the transgender and genderfluid communities themselves. I can't tell you how many posts I see a day, written on the countless genderfluid Facebook groups and forums of which I am a member, by genderfluid individuals, detailing the now-stereotypical two juxtaposed pictures of an individual's "masculine vs. feminine" or "boy vs. girl" days. I digest these posts as a normative perpetuation of cisgender stereotypes. That's not to say that genderfluid identities that consist of binary genders or binary presentations should be discredited: they should not. Unfortunately, we live in a society in which in order to be seen "as a girl" or "as feminine" or as one gender or another, you're limited to how far you can stretch that presentation, otherwise people will discredit your gender identity. Nonetheless, this realization is just another symptom of harmful policing and stereotyping. Because I'm caught in the swirling chaos of cisgendernormativity I cannot seem to eschew, I, like many other genderfluid and nonbinary people, am stuck in this paradox of contending dualities: how I perceive myself and my gender(s) versus how others perceive my gender(s).

As an aside, more often than not, these posts are framed as dichotomized boy/girl, and I can't help but note the wording implies an infantile undertone (using boy instead of man, girl instead of woman), as if identity is something you have to work for or grow into, rather than something you are.

Now, pronouns: such a significant factor, so integral to gender identity, yet such a simple form of legitimate validation. When I decided to transition from primarily using *she/her* to *they/them* as pronouns, I was unsure how some of my friends would receive this news. It took me a while to come to the conclusion that I wanted to primarily use *they/them* in the first place. However, almost every family member and friend I've approached about pronouns was supportive, and when people use them as I request, I feel amazing. I feel legitimate. I feel valid, and I feel all the better because my friends support and recognize my identity in a very legitimate way. Being validated by other people spurs me to want to validate myself. Because I don't use "traditional" binary pronouns (*he/him, she/her*), it's often easy for strangers to scoff or ignore them. The most common criticism I see for people unsupportive of *they/them* as nonbinary pronouns is the claim that *they/them* is not grammatically correct. Well, naysayers, take a closer look: the American Dialect Society declared the singular pronoun *they* Word of the Year for 2015 (Guo, 2016). Katy Steinmetz, of *Time Magazine*, declares that this validation of *they* as a singular pronoun has the potential to "jolt people into second-guessing some of the assumptions society has long had about gender – about all hims and all hers, about what destiny is really in store for any baby who is proclaimed to be a boy or a girl in the delivery room" (Steinmetz, 2016). My pronouns, *they* pronouns, are just as valid as anyone else's, and this declaration of *they* as Word of the Year will jettison this legitimacy into the spotlight and hopefully give those condescending, self-proclaimed grammar nerds something to think about.

Transitioning from one form of policing to another, this focus on controlling acceptable genderfluid and transgender presentation is ever pertinent, as with renewed determination, certain states in the U.S. are making headway with regards to transgender civil rights. The Massachusetts State Bathroom Bill, formally known as House Bill 1577, had been up for consideration: the bill seeks to "amend the language in current state law to protect transgender people from being discriminated in public places" (Martinez, 2015). The Massachusetts Senate overwhelmingly voted to pass this Bathroom Bill, meaning that this legislation, extending full protections and providing anti-discrimination policies under the law to transgender Bay Staters, will allow "transgender people to use the public restroom consistent with their gender identity" (Dumcius, 2016). Moreover, the purpose of the bill is to extend acceptance of transgender people in all public accommodations, writes Joshua Miller of *The Boston Globe* staff, such as in "sports arenas, gas stations, movie theaters, bars, malls, and other public accommodations… It would specifically allow people to use the restrooms, locker rooms, and changing rooms that match their gender identity" (2016). I am ecstatic to announce that as I pen this paragraph, on the evening of June 1st, 2016, Massachusetts' House of Representatives voted to pass this public accommodations bill – a landmark decision in transgender rights (Miller, 2016)! The bill will be written into law as soon as Massachusetts Governor Charlie Baker signs it.

As with any civil rights bill perceived by protesters are "controversial," backlash continues to abound with fury. The most common argument opponents claim is that "male sexual predators, under the guise of being transgender, could enter women's restrooms and locker rooms" (Miller, 2016). Protesters of this bill have gone so far as to formulate petitions lashing out at proponents and supporters of the bill, some of which are retailers and large companies. One such petition is that of the American Family Association (AFA), a conservative activist group, against the retailer Target (Malcolm 2016). Target recently announced that transgender customers and workers can use the bathroom that aligns with the gender with which they identify (Wahba, 2016). The retailer's stance was clear. In response, a protest erupted, along with the surfacing hashtag #BoycottTarget. As of April 28th, 2016, over 700,000 people signed this petition, pledging to boycott Target over its transgender-inclusive bathroom policy (Malcolm, 2016). Writes Phil Wahba, contributor to *Forbes*, Target held steadfast to this inclusive policy, though the aforementioned AFA petition eventually climbed to 973,000 people (2016).

These outrageous protestations are inextricably linked to the policing of gender presentation, as executed by the cisgender populace and its cis-centric ideology. I have bared witness to more than one Facebook rant regarding the Bathroom Bill, complete with bigotry and transmisogyny in the comments. The assumption of these protesters is that your genitals, and moreover your entire physical body and how you present that body, define your gender. I've seen countless cisgender people on the web air their concerns about the bill, claiming they don't want a "man in woman's clothing to sneak into the women's restroom, intent on harassment," or vice versa, and other nonsense remarks along these lines. This negativity is slung especially at transwomen and transfeminine individuals. Unlike the transphobic assumptions to which these protesters lay claim, a transwoman is not a "man dressing as a woman" or a "former man" or "someone who used to be a guy." Transwomen are women, period. As women, they deserve the right to use the women's restroom if they choose, and they deserve to feel safe in doing so. Regardless of gender presentation, one should be able to feel comfortable and confident in using the restroom to which they want to go. To police bathroom access is to police identity, and to police identity is to restrict acceptable representations of that identity – gender expression.

A recent unsettling encounter convinced me that the uninformed public tends not to take serious transgender safety in public restrooms. On one occasion this summer, I chose to wait in the impossibly long line to the women's restroom at a park at Old Orchard Beach, Maine. A woman decided to hop the "ladies" line and follow her husband into the men's restroom. After noticing the awkward stares of the people still waiting in both bathroom lines, her husband, half-laughing exclaimed, "Haha it's okay! She identifies as a man, so she can go in here!" The lady behind me in the line laughed in approval, nodded, and said, "That's all it takes these days!" intimating that acceptable access to either restroom can be easily approved or dismissed. As evidenced by this anecdote, many people perceive trans equality as a joke, despite the violence and continual micro-aggressions trans people face on a daily basis.

I fear public restrooms, even at work – an otherwise friendly environment. As someone who is nonbinary genderfluid, I imagine I am not alone in feeling uncomfortable using both men's and women's restrooms. This unease stems from the realization that my gender presentation is often not clocked as feminine or "female," nor do I think it would be acceptable for me to use the men's restroom, as I don't quite pass as a guy. I usually get in and out as fast as possible, avoiding the eyes of others in the restroom. My discomfort lies in the possibility that people will question why I am using either restroom. Because I am nonbinary, no matter my current gender, I'm always left with the sinking feeling that my presentation isn't "normal" enough for my circumstances. It's increasingly critical that public accommodations should all have at least one unisex bathroom for this reason. I use unisex restrooms whenever I can, eschewing what otherwise appear to be binary restrooms. So, unless I use the few-and-far-between unisex bathrooms, I feel the pressure and obligation to present so I "pass" in one restroom or the other.

The conclusion remains thus: assumptions about one's gender based on presentation reinforce the standards to which that gender should be judged, and therefore, accepted by cisgender onlookers. There presents itself an expectation that your gender presentation should *clearly* represent the cisnormative representation of that gender, an oppressive force insisting your gender should "match" the presentation of how that gender is perceived. Gender cannot, and should not, be reduced to gender expression. The policing of gender expression, especially nonbinary genderfluid gender presentation, creates a disruption between an individual's identity and how that identity is perceived. Genderfluid presentation cannot, and indeed *should not*, be misconstrued and reduced to various composite binary identities and expressions. The very binarization which my genderfluid identity seeks to transcend continues to nonetheless drag me down into the wake of cisheteronormative expression. We who have a voice must continuously battle against those who seek to dismantle, demean, and dissect our identities. We are the next generation of gender outlaws.

DISCUSSION QUESTIONS

1. Define gender identity.
2. How do you perceive masculinity? Femininity? How do these perceptions inform your gender? Do these perceptions inform the assumption you make of others' genders?
3. How do you define the term "man?" "Woman?"
4. Describe the differences between binary and nonbinary gender.
5. How do you define and express your gender identity?
6. How do Judith Butler's views on gender and gender theory relate to gender nonconforming identities? Does one inform the other?
7. Why do you think genderfluid and gender nonconforming individuals continue to face prejudice and marginalization, given the apparent rise in support for the LGBTQ and MOGAI communities?
8. What types of gender stereotypes do you encounter in your country?
9. How many transgender characters have you encountered in pop culture? Actors? Actresses?

SUGGESTED RESOURCES

Adrian Ballou, "10 Myths About Non-Binary People It's Time to Unlearn". http://everydayfeminism.com/2014/12/myths-non-binary-people/

Avinash Chak, "Beyond 'he' and 'she': The rise of non-binary pronouns". http://www.bbc.com/news/magazine-34901704

BAGLY (Boston Alliance of Gay, Lesbian, Bisexual, Transgender Youth). http://www.bagly.org/

Boston Pride: http://www.bostonpride.org/

GenderqueerID.com: http://genderqueerid.com/

Gender Diversity: Terminology: http://www.genderdiversity.org/resources/terminology/

Human Rights Campaign: http://www.hrc.org/

Judith Butler (1990). *Gender Trouble: Feminism and the Subversion of Identity*. New York: Routledge. doi:http://lauragonzalez.com/TC/BUTLER_gender_trouble.pdf

Kate Borenstein and S. Bear Bergman, *Gender Outlaws: The Next Generation.*

Laura Erickson-Schroth (Ed.), *Trans Bodies, Trans Selves: A Resource for the Transgender Community.*

REFERENCES

Dumcius, G. (2016, May 02). *Massachusetts lawmakers advance transgender anti-discrimination legislation.* Retrieved from http://www.masslive.com/politics/index.ssf/2016/05/massachusetts_lawmakers_advanc.html

Guo, J. (2016, January 8). *Sorry, grammar nerds. The singular 'they' has been declared word of the Year.* Retrieved from https://www.washingtonpost.com/news/wonk/wp/2016/01/08/donald-trump-may-win-this-years-word-of-the-year/

Malcolm, H. (2016, April 28). *More than 500,000 boycott target over transgender bathroom policy.* Retrieved from http://www.usatoday.com/story/money/2016/04/25/conservative-christian-group-boycotting-target-transgender-bathroom-policy/83491396/

Martinez, A. (2015, November 12). *Transgender rights: MA lawmakers push for "Bathroom Bill".* Retrieved from http://wwlp.com/2015/11/12/transgender-rights-ma-lawmakers-push-for-bathroom-bill/

Miller, J. (2016, May 12). Mass: Senate passes transgender bill. *The Boston Globe.* Retrieved from https://www.bostonglobe.com/metro/2016/05/12/massachusetts-senate-poised-pass-transgender-bill/vD2x4VifOmNuBGiCSNXAkL/story.html

Miller, J. (2016, June 1). House passes transgender bill after heated debate. *The Boston Globe.* Retrieved from https://www.bostonglobe.com/metro/2016/06/01/house-passes-transgender-bill/tgGBBY3xiu2BqlhPgQY2rO/story.html

Steinmetz, K. (2016, January 8). This pronoun is the word of the year for 2015. *Time Magazine.* Retrieved from http://time.com/4173992/word-of-the-year-2015-they/

Wahba, P. (2016, April 28). *Nearly 1 million sign pledge to boycott target over bathroom policy.* Retrieved from http://fortune.com/2016/04/28/target-transgender-bathroom-petition/

15. TITANIUM TITS

I'm going to go out on a limb here, and say that middle school is the worst.

Informal polls, which I've taken across various gender, ethnic, age, and religious groups, in person and on social media, confirm that my own experience (which was the worst) may have been, if not universal, at least representative, in mood if not in details. Each of us has had a different subjective experience, a particular family culture, distinctive friends, and various layers to our respective identities. One thing appears to be true: being fourteen sucks.

When I was in eighth grade, aged fourteen, I experienced my first true existential crisis, something that would recur throughout my adolescence and adulthood, and which sometimes strikes me now, though I'm much older and ostensibly wiser – even more so than I was a year ago, but we'll get to that. A particular adolescent spell of what I now call "paradoxical nihilism," featuring a peculiar blend of thinking nothing mattered and feeling as if everything did, was sparked by three things that occurred within the span of a week: my first concussion, a kind of creeping awareness that maybe I wasn't straight, and a comment made by a boy who, until the moment he walked by my lunch table and called me a name, I had considered a friend.

In fact, I'd stood up for that boy, way back in third grade when he was substantially overweight and the butt of playground jokes. He invited me to his ninth birthday party, which was held in what my mom called a "bad part of town," and which featured a screening of *The Lost Boys*, an eighties vampire movie that was rated R and thus *verboten* in my house. I remember getting about halfway through the movie when my parents arrived to pick me up – we must have had some sort of dinner plans – and not telling them anything about it ("lying through omission" is what my dad would label the same behavior, many years later).

His apartment – he was one of my only friends who lived in an apartment and not a house – was literally on the other side of the railroad tracks, far beyond my permitted bike-riding radius. His single mom, who had too-tan

P. Leavy (Ed.), Privilege Through the Looking-Glass, 103–114.
© *2017 Sense Publishers. All rights reserved.*

skin and bottle-blonde hair and was never without a cigarette and, I learned later, a bottle of vodka, hadn't bothered to decorate, beyond one sad streamer that hung, flaccid, above the front door. We sang "Happy Birthday;" we ate a Dairy Queen cake; we made microwave popcorn before we settled in for the movie.

Only Michael, who became a bouncer at a local bar in his adulthood, his friend David, who would go on to start a goth band, a couple of younger kids from down the street, and I showed up for the party.

He'd invited our whole class.

***

Western philosophy, with which I had an academic love affair that lasted many years, and which may or may not have been a waste of my time, has spent a good while trying to figure out What It All Means. Beginning roughly with the guys before Socrates and extending through still-active philosophers such as Judith Butler, Gilles Deleuze, and bell hooks, What It All Means is at the core. Some write in more accessible ways than others, but the basic impulse is the same: *question things.*[1]

When I was in graduate school, I went down the rabbit hole of postmodernism and post-structuralism, both theoretical apparatuses designed to confuse and confound, two different kinds of intellectual hijinks that led, at least in my case, to overt nihilism of the unpleasantly cynical – not paradoxical or even cautiously optimistic – variety. Being a graduate student at a well-respected university comes with its own sorts of privileges, such as access to money, the acquisition of unquestioned cultural capital, (paid) time to read books and write about them, and the requisite accompanying arrogance, but being aware of that doesn't matter to many privileged, intellectually promiscuous twenty-somethings who want to live a life of the mind (or whatever we're calling it these days).

Awareness, at least of the kind that has any meaning at all, was lost on me for a while until the year I wrote my dissertation – a very long document that cites many of the aforementioned confusing and confounding philosophers in its quest to dismantle what we think we know about all kinds of things – much too quickly. Then I decided to become a novelist instead. That didn't quite work out, at least not in a way that pays the bills, which led to another crisis, this one more severe than the last (they seem to get worse, albeit less frequent, as time goes on). Was I good enough? Was I lying to myself? What did it all mean, anyway? Not for the first time in my existence, I'd been leading a double life: by day, I was a diligent graduate student, working to meet my degree requirements so that I could graduate on time and get the prized academic job. But by night, I thrilled myself by writing mystery fiction, where I thought I could make a difference in some kind of concrete way, which felt opposed to the absence of difference I might make in my scholarly pursuits. It did not compute, and I may have gone a little crazy for a couple of years.

What is an existential crisis, you might ask? I can sum it up with one noun, and I do so with the awareness that existential crises, like most things, are subjective: *angst*. Angst that awakens you from a deep sleep with a surge of adrenaline. Angst that makes you wonder what would happen if, on the highway at eighty miles an hour, you cut the wheel sharply to the left and into oncoming traffic, but that simultaneously stops you from finding out.

***

I got the eighth-grade concussion on a Monday night, along with a dose of whiplash; a horse threw me, and I landed on my head and neck. My mom took me to the emergency room, where the doctor announced that I wasn't allowed to sleep for longer than an hour at a time until twenty-four hours had passed, lest my brain swell inside of my skull until I was no more.

***

"Titanium tits".

That's what Michael called me that Wednesday, the day I returned to school after the horseback riding incident. I was sitting with a couple of friends, whose names and faces elude me now, though I'm certain that one of them was making fun of "Skittles" – a boy who in retrospect was obviously on the autistic spectrum and whose mother cut his hair the best she could – while the other listened to my impressive medical drama.

The conversation waned and I gazed at the flickering florescent glow of the vending machine, chomped my cheese sandwich, took a sip of my fruit punch, and wondered whether my neck would stop hurting at some point.

I saw David, for whom puberty was unkind in every perceptible way, come around the corner first, followed by Michael, who at fourteen was very close to his adult height of six-two, and who had converted what people like grandmothers call "baby fat" into a thick combination of muscle and sinew, which he adorned with cut-off black Dickies, a chain wallet, a tattered black T-shirt, and a pair of combat boots. Michael seemed cool and vaguely threatening to me; he didn't come to school often, and when he did he spent most of the time smoking on the railroad tracks behind the building, back behind the bushes where he thought no one could see him.

"Titanium tits," he mumbled to his acne-faced friend, his figure hulking in front of the vending machine, his index finger pointed in my direction. I looked around and realized that he was talking about me.

"What?" I squawked, surprised and embarrassed, because my now-faceless friends at the table were trying not to laugh. I looked down at my breasts. They looked fine to me. I saw no evidence of exposed nipple or asymmetry.

"Yup. Titanium. Tits," he said again, louder the second time, better-enunciated, as David covered his face with his hand and snorted.

Michael pointed at me one last time, chuckled, and then turned to Skittles and said something rude about his haircut.

I got up, threw the rest of my lunch in the trash, and walked away, pissed at my friends for not helping me, hoping that "Titanium Tits" wasn't going to become some kind of semi-permanent nickname.

***

I got a chain wallet and some black T-shirts and shaved part of my head, but I had a hard time aligning my desire to be punk-rock-cool with my love of horseback riding. For a while, I led what felt like a double life, until I outgrew horses all together.

***

Later in my eighth-grade year, a different boy groped my titanium tits after cornering me during gym class, an action that I recognized as sinister and vaguely threatening. I think it was the look on his face, a menacing stare at my left breast as he reached out to squeeze the right, his tongue flicking across his lips to moisten them. Or it could have been the way he leaned into me, my breast still in his hand, whispering that I had "such nice titties," titties he'd like to see, before giving it a final squeeze and walking away. Or it could have been the fact that I didn't want him to touch me and he did it anyway.

I had been wearing a new bra that day, one that was lightly padded and made me feel pretty and as feminine as I'd ever felt under my rock-and-roll T-shirts and jeans, and while I suppose a part of me appreciated the attention, another part of me, the deep-down reptile brain, was terrified. I remember standing there, right where he'd left me, frozen, until I quietly retreated into the locker room.

I'd never spoken to that boy before, and after my mom called the principal following a difficult conversation – I learned then that shame makes my hands shake when I speak – I didn't see the boy at school again. I heard later that he'd been expelled, because my titanium tits weren't his first grope.

***

The existentialists, a group of philosophers, writers, and artists who were active in Europe roughly at the turn of the twentieth century, believed that humans make their own meaning, that we struggle to be rational in spite of the fact that the universe itself is irrational. I've always struggled to make meaning, and I'm no longer convinced that being rational ought to be a goal in life; sometimes irrationality is better. Because when people toss words like "fag" and "dyke" and "nigger" around while other people go on television and proclaim that it would be a good idea to build a big wall between the United States and Mexico, people like me come along and try to figure out What It All Means, and people like me end up in crisis.

At the end of the day, Jean-Paul Sartre thought, what matters isn't what it means, or even what we believe. What matters is how we behave, what we do, how we love.

***

The first time someone called me a dyke was also in eighth grade, in that same damnable lunchroom, right after I showed my punk-rock pride by buying my first pair of Doc Martens. I decided pretty quickly that I didn't like how it felt to be named, categorized in so crass a manner, so I got a boyfriend – a series of them, actually, several of them serious – and decided that I would be heterosexual. It was a real decision, something about which I'd written reams of bad poetry and pages in my journal. It wasn't anything I told anyone, either. It was my secret, and keeping it gave me what I thought was power.

It took me a long time to understand that the only way I could feel any power at all was by being as authentic as I could be, so I came out at twenty-five, after I fell in love with the woman who is now my wife. When I told my mom, my hands didn't shake.

***

Last year, I was working out at the gym when a man wanted to use the piece of equipment I was using. Instead of waiting his turn, he called me "such a cute dyke" and walked away.

I still don't like how that word makes me feel.

How does he know? I wondered. I didn't ask my wife, who was also my lifting partner, what she thought. I just got angry. So angry that my face turned purple and a couple of other people asked me if I was okay. I lied and said that I was, and then I squatted more than I had in recent months.

I was so angry that over a year has passed and I still remember it like it was yesterday, only now the anger has turned back into hurt, not because of what he said, but because it mattered enough to him to say it. Because it revealed that I'm not fooling anyone after all; it eroded what I thought was safety, shrouded in straight privilege.

It makes another scar, albeit one that isn't quite as visible as the ones on my skin are.

***

I'm a word person, and I've been thinking a lot about the word "privilege" lately, for reasons that we can see all over the media. To get specific, I'm originally from northeast Ohio and I write mystery fiction set in Cleveland; relatively recent events with the Cleveland police and the African-American community (read: cops regularly beating and shooting black people, often mentally ill black people, with few or no consequences), combined with my ongoing research interest in crime and crime fighting, has led me to read a lot, itself an example of the privilege of the highly literate. I've read documents from the Department of Justice about police behavior (we don't call it "brutality" anymore) and lot of newspaper articles. A lot of comments on those articles, likely written by able-bodied and able-minded white people, mostly men, suggest the opposite of awareness: those people, with their thinly veiled racism, write with almost gleeful, dare I say blissful, ignorance, and the rhetorician in me wants to jump in and correct their feeble logic, knowing full well that it won't matter if I do.

I'm privileged: I'm a thirty-something, middle-class, highly educated white woman with a partner (and, therefore, a two-income household), parents who have always loved and supported me, good health insurance, a reliable car, and a full-time academic job that lets me – even wants me – to write essays such as this one. I can pay my mortgage on a house in a nice, quiet neighborhood. I can pay for a gym membership and have the good fortune to have time to use it. I can afford to get my car fixed if one of the potholes in my riddled state shatters a ball joint. This is the reality. As is the fact that so much of this makes that guy at the gym sound like an inconsequential rube, like an ignoramus who belongs in line behind myriad internet trolls, but whose palpable hatred has real social and economic consequences for anyone who is poor or black or brown or mentally ill or disabled or trans or fat, but not for me.

It makes me wonder what it would be like to be black or brown or trans or fat, what kinds of things other people – other humans – experience every single day, and how they make meaning out of hate.

***

In the interest of coming full-circle here, I should add that my straight privilege, or whatever shred of it I thought I had, eroded almost completely not long ago, right around the time that jerk at the gym made his comment.

My titanium tits tried to kill me (aggressive breast cancer at thirty-six can and does happen, even to people who eat natural foods and exercise), so I had them amputated. Those scars on my skin that I mentioned earlier are real; there are four of them, four places where the surgeon's scalpel sliced me to save my life, and they mark my white chest with raised, pink lines. I'm told that they'll fade over time, but I'm not sure I want them to; even as specters of the breasts that are now gone, they remind me of what I have.

I'm not transgender, but I imagine these days that some folks think I am, especially at first glance and from a distance. I have short hair and no breasts, and that confuses people. I've always been sensitive enough, at least since my high school experiment with shaving my entire head (and not just half), to know that hair matters, whether we like it or not. So I kept mine unique; of course I had what a friend of mine calls an "alternative lifestyle haircut," but it was still feminine. I could claim my punk-rock roots or something. During and following chemotherapy, not so much. I just looked like a dyke, at least when I didn't look like a cancer patient anymore, and I found that my own internalized homophobia is far more pernicious than I thought it was.

I don't want to look like a dyke; I want to look like me. These days I often wear a lightly padded bra-like thing or prosthetic breasts, which I call "foobs" and pretend to be good-natured about, mostly because I don't appreciate people gawking at me when I'm shopping at the home-improvement store or grading papers at the coffee shop.

Whether they really gawk at me or it's all in my head is a matter of subjective opinion.

What all of this reveals to me, good post-structuralist that I am, is that words both contain power and have no power.[2] "Dyke" signifies something different to me than it does the asshole at the gym a year ago; but, both ways, it's an epithet. It's meant to injure. But I'm already injured by something that is both more concrete and more abstract: the tumor had to be removed before it ravaged my body and ended my life, and even if the scars fade, I wonder whether the cancer itself will ever cease to be another specter, something that haunts me, something that wakes me at night with a jolt of adrenaline.

***

I think about clichés a lot. As a writer and a writing teacher, avoiding the cliché is at the top of my agenda a lot of the time. In my first novel, which as of now remains unpublished, my protagonist – who is not my double, in spite of the fact that some readers seem unable to grasp that fiction is not memoir – laments the fact that she's become a cliché –but here's the takeaway point: clichés and their sociological sisters, stereotypes, exist for a reason. When applied to large groups of people, they often hold. This isn't something that I like to acknowledge, but I – and we – don't do anyone any favors by pretending that it isn't the case.

We get into trouble when we start to apply clichés and/or stereotypes to individual people. That isn't how sociology, even bad sociology, works. And, frankly, it's not how life works.

We all know people who fall into what I like to call "characters from central casting." Think about the blue-collar worker who drinks too much beer. The white-collar worker who defrauds his own company. The too-tan, vodka-swilling single mom who lets her nine-year-old watch *The Lost Boys* because she's too tired to care. The formerly-fat kid who grew up to be a bouncer at a bar. The nineties queer-mo cancer patient who is now a writing professor.

But what about the racist asshole who guns down an innocent black man? He guns down that black man *because of stereotypes*, but that action makes the gunman a stereotype, too. It makes him a cliché. And this is an uncomfortable truth, especially for those of us interested in social justice who are sick and tired of this crap. But it's a truth nevertheless.

***

About a year ago, my partner and I were meandering through the then-new natural foods store in town, filling our cart with things like basil-goat-cheese dip, sprouted-grain tortillas, craft beer, and fancy sparkling water. As I combed the bulk aisle for the perfect trail mix, it hit me: *I'm a middle-aged, middle-class, cisgender white woman, and my privilege is in that shopping cart.*

In that moment, I realized what had been one of my worst fears: I'm a cliché. At least we don't have a Subaru with a Coexist sticker, but we're damn close. I'm a professor; she's a gardener. We consider our pets our kids, and now that we've gotten through the Very Bad Year that breast cancer wrought, we're thinking about having an actual kid. We can do this because, in spite of the ways in which we *don't* have privilege, there are many, many ways in which we *do* have it.

"Titanium tits" and "dyke" be damned: we're still privileged.

***

I'll never forget that summer day, after I'd had a needle jammed into me a few times, when I saw the tubes of flesh – my flesh, my tumor, my own DNA gone bonkers – floating in formalin. "Want to see?" the nurse asked. And, of course, I did want to see, because I've never been one to look away.

People who have had a serious illness often write about how they divide their lives in two, marked with the temporal "before" and "after." This is philosophically complicated, but I look at it this way: chronic illness brings mortality – the awareness of which most humans smartly relegate to the backs of their minds – into the light. Mortality, and attempting to make it less immanent, has the power to trigger yet another existential crisis, far beyond what "titanium tits" or "dyke" might elicit. Looking down the barrel of one's own demise is terrifying.

But that's beyond the scope of my point, here. Before, I could fly under the radar if I wanted; I could pass however I wanted to pass to avoid making people uncomfortable. To avoid rocking the boat. To save myself the pain of being accosted outside of a public restroom by what would likely be a white man with some kind of complex; to save myself the embarrassment of being misgendered in public. It sucks. I'd rather wear foobs.

Titanium tits.

***

At the end of it all, here's where I stand: I might be a cancer warrior (I can't stand the term "survivor" in this context, because everyone, everywhere is "surviving"), but I'm also a highly-educated (some would say over-educated), middle-class white woman. I made it through eighth grade; I made it through graduate school; I came out of the philosophical rabbit-hole and now I'm employed by a large state university in the Midwest; my partner, with whom I traded titanium wedding bands two years ago, and I own a home; I have a decent car; I go to the gym; I do yoga; I eat healthy food; I'm writing this on a newish computer that does what I want it to do; I have health care that pays for the myriad medical procedures that I endure on a semi-regular basis and that also pays for me to see a therapist – and by now it's probably pretty clear that me seeing a therapist is a good idea. My titanium tits have been, at least so far (knock wood), unsuccessful in their attempt to pluck me from this planet; my hair is back; I no longer wear the pallor of the sick.

Maybe more important in this context is this fact: if I get pulled over by the police, it's unlikely that it will end in violence. It's far more likely that other white folks will take issue with things that I address in the fiction that I write; the novel that's underway these days takes our brave protagonist, herself a police detective, into the world of institutionalized racism. It's me doing what I can do, in the name of social justice and for my personal well-being. Existential crisis be damned: I'm a writer, and writers write.

***

These days, I identify more with the Stoics than I do with Derrida, though I'd still classify myself as an existentialist at heart. Language makes for fun games, but I care more about being a decent human being than I do about being perceived as an intellectual contender. How I behave matters more than how well I string words together.

But it takes language for me to express that, language that slips and slides and means something different depending on one's own sense of identity. It's a paradox.

***

Michael, last I heard, is still a bouncer at that crappy dive bar in my hometown. I'd bet all of the money in my checking account that he doesn't remember that moment, in eighth grade, when his clever use of alliteration led me into an early brush with angst. I'd bet that the jackass at the gym doesn't remember me, either, and certainly not what he said to me, because that's how privilege works: we assert it without knowing what we're doing. We toss it around out of ignorance, but it has the power to injure in ways that parallel a surgeon's ten-blade. The question is whether our psyches heal as impressively as our bodies do.

DISCUSSION QUESTIONS

1. How do you define "privilege"? Does it upset you when others' privileges get in the way of your own goals?
2. Make a list of all the ways in which you're oppressed. Go into detail. Then make a list of all of the ways in which you're privileged. Do you

see patterns emerging? Share with your peers, compare lists, and discuss your findings.

3. Which of your own privileges have you earned? Are any of them unearned? How do you understand the distinction between the two forms of privilege?

4. What representative examples of early adolescence exist in popular culture? Why is it, for example, that high school narratives seem to take precedence over middle school narratives? Are these representations accurate? Why or why not? What do they leave out, and why do they omit those things?

5. What cultural representations of existential crises can you find and identify? Are these representations accurate? Why or why not?

WRITING PROMPTS

1. What were your middle school experiences? Did you experience any discrimination or privilege? What did that look like for you?

2. Using your list of privileges (see above) as a starting point, identify a subculture to which you do not belong. Research that subculture, paying special attention to the ways in which that subculture is oppressed by mainstream contemporary culture and what issues its members face as a result of that oppression. Explain the issue(s) and take a position on it/them. Write a research(ed) essay that works through 2–3 carefully constructed research questions that you design.

3. Then, switch into a more creative gear. Explain and take a position on the issue(s) from the perspective of someone who belongs to the subculture. Your research should guide you to a place where you develop new insights; this second part should be a focused fictional narrative, where you take on the position of someone who belongs in the group. Write this in the first person.

4. Select one of the above-named philosophical schools of thought (existentialism, Stoicism, post-structuralism, postmodernism) and do some exploring. Write a description of what you find, and translate what you've learned into layperson's terms. What Does It Mean, especially in the context of privilege?

NOTES

[1] For more, I suggest starting with the online *Stanford Encyclopedia of Philosophy*, which does a good job of making What It All Means accessible. There's also a remarkably good

novel by Jostein Gardner called *Sophie's World*, which I read as an undergrad philosophy major, way back when, and which will show you the history of Western philosophy in a creative way.

2   This is the essence of post-structuralism, a complicated series of language games that asserts, among other things, that nothing but a reader exists outside of a text. For example, for a post-structuralist, this essay exists on its own, as a string of words put together by an author who relinquishes her power to you, the reader, who is largely constructed by the culture in which you live. Any meaning that you find here is made by you, not me. The big names in this school of thought are Jacques Derrida, Julia Kristeva, Gilles Deleuze, and Michel Foucault.

LISA BARRY

16. ON NOT BEING A VICTORIA'S SECRET MODEL

A Critical Analysis of My Struggle with Social Comparison and Objectification

That's sad. How plastic and artificial life has become. It gets harder and harder to find something ... real.

(Scott, 2011, p. 85)

He held up the Victoria's Secret catalog and said, "How come you never dress like that?" Really? I wanted to kick him in the face.

Instead, I gathered myself and, very calmly, said, "I teach. And we have a dress code. That would be inappropriate".

"Well, what about on the weekends?"

"On the weekends, I want to relax. I don't want to have to dress up."

"Not even for me?"

"I'd like to think you love me for who I am, not how I dress."

"So you don't want to dress like that?"

"No."

"Well you should."

He ultimately left me for a tall, leggy blonde. She was my best friend, or so I thought. They were sleeping together behind my back. I wonder if she dressed like that?

I couldn't articulate at the time why I felt so uncomfortable. And angry. I was midway through my master's degree and was only truly beginning to immerse myself in the various theoretical approaches to communication, both rhetorical and social scientific. I was also only beginning to become aware of and comfortable with my feminist self.

A few years later, as I worked toward my doctoral degree, I stumbled across Sut Jhally's (1997) *Dreamworlds 2: Desire, Sex, Power in Music Video*. Shortly after I saw what was for me a ground-breaking and mind-opening articulation of all the things in my head about the portrayal of women in American media, I saw Britney Spears' "(Hit Me Baby) One More Time." Jhally's insistence that the dreamworld of the music video

P. Leavy (Ed.), Privilege Through the Looking-Glass, 115–124.

represents adolescent male fantasies, one of which is schoolgirls, and my sudden recognition that this music video was exactly what he was talking about literally shocked me into becoming a fairly well-articulated feminist being. At the same time, I struggled because, unlike many feminists of the time (or so I thought, based on my readings of feminist theory about the role of motherhood as a patriarchal construction), I did not fit the mold of a traditional feminist. As the single mother of a six-year-old son, I not only embraced, but enjoyed my role as a mother. On top of that, I was attracted to men (I still am), so I rejected the notion that motherhood is a form of patriarchal domination.

Although a few scholars acknowledged that single motherhood could be a choice, I argued single motherhood is a form of resistance to patriarchal domination. I actually viewed single motherhood as a means to empower women. I did not see myself as a victim, but rather as a warrior, as someone who challenged the notion that single motherhood is an obstacle to success. My son was my motivation to complete my degree in record time and to prove to the world that single mothers can be beautiful, successful, intelligent, articulate, and proud. I was clearly intelligent and articulate. I was on my way to being successful. But I definitely did not feel beautiful. Nor did I feel proud. Instead, I felt like a loser as a woman, utterly unattractive and undesirable, simply because I was not a Victoria's Secret model and had been told I should be.

I have always been curvy. Well, not always. I always had a small waist and proportional hips, but I didn't get breasts until the summer before my senior year in high school. I went from a 32AA to a 32C in a matter of months. And because I always spent summers in California visiting my father, the difference in my body was especially noticeable for the 375 or so kids at my small, Colorado ski town high school. The rumor was that I'd had a boob job. Did people do that back then? In 1981? I'm not sure they did. The "Twiggy" look was still in. I think. Anyway, I was a "perfect 34" by the time I finally went to college when I was 23. I had been a gymnast and a dancer all my life, and nothing changed in college except for the gymnastics. I did dance theatre instead. I loved it. I had a great body: muscular, toned, curvy, perfect dimensions. Dark hair. Dark eyes. A sultry Scorpio. Everything a guy would want, right?

The problem is that I'm short. All my life I wanted to be 5'4" but I never made it. I was 5'3" on a good day if I stood up really tall, which was good for gymnastics and dance, actually. I was more agile, had lower clearance, and was less likely to fall (or fall far). I think I'm shrinking. I'm more like 5'2" now.

A Victoria's Secret model I'm not. Never was. Never will be. Don't want to be, actually. I'm not a tall, leggy blonde. I'm neither tall, nor leggy, and I'll sure as hell never dye my hair blonde. I'm short, curvy, highly educated, and highly intelligent. Three strikes against me as a woman, at least for most men I've ever known or been attracted to. Add to that the fact that I've been a single mom my son's entire life (and he's now in a doctoral program), and you can count me out. Four strikes. I'm everything men don't want. Well, men my age, anyway. I think men my age are afraid of me, actually. I'm outspoken and passionate. Another strike. The problem was, I was beautiful...I just didn't know it.

After years of research and writing about images of women in American media, I realized that I fall victim to what is often referenced in objectification theory and/or social comparison theory. Not the theories themselves, but the behaviors and thoughts that form the basis for the theories. I first began to articulate those thoughts and feelings in my first tenure-track position, where I developed and taught a course in Visual Communication, the foundation for which I grounded in John Berger's (1972) landmark discussion of the similarity between classical images of the nude and contemporary advertising.

Berger (1972) argues that just as the spectator for classical oil paintings of the nude was assumed to be male so, too, is the contemporary spectator-consumer assumed to be male; women's images are used to appeal to him. Sut Jhally, in all incarnations including the most recent *Dreamworlds* (2010), offers the same argument about music videos. A similar understanding of women's objectivity and of spectatorship, common in feminist film theory and criticism, emerged during the second wave of the Women's Movement in the late 1960s and early 1970s. In the early decades, the movement focused on giving women a voice and striving for equality in all areas of society – domestic as well as public. Feminist film theory and criticism initially examined the various ways film reinforced the more traditional images of women. These "image studies" examined the cinematic depiction of women from a sociological perspective, identified how female characters were often stereotyped, and attempted to determine whether or not female characters offered positive or negative role models for their audiences. Shortly after, another form of criticism emerged in which critics studied the use of signs and symbols and argued that women signify the object of male desire in Hollywood film. This psychoanalytic perspective became the norm for much of the field of feminist film criticism and still influences such analyses today. Closely linked with Berger's and Jhally's discussions of the woman as object and male as spectator, this psychoanalytic perspective illuminates how the spectator is situated in relation to the object – whether as women on screen or as nudes on a canvas.

The article most closely related to Berger's (1972) and Jhally's (1997, 2010) works is likely an article by Ann Simonton (1995) titled "Women for Sale." This essay exposes the link between advertising's way of seeing women and actual violence against women. She grounds her argument in Berger's, and claims, "Women in advertising are portrayed as being keenly aware of the fact that they are being watched and judged… She performs a relentless surveillance – is she having a bad hair day, is there a run in her hose, lipstick bleed, oily nose, chipped nail – is she too fat?" (p. 149). Simonton believes women transform themselves for men's approval and men constitute the dominant culture. She concludes, "The biggest barrier to social equality may be that many women have become unwittingly attached to the woman who is on sale and on display" (p. 161). Display, she claims, works to dehumanize, objectify, and victimize women.

This display is much like that described by Berger and Jhally. Display assumes spectatorship, assumes somebody is looking, even if it is the woman herself. Berger neatly sums up women's role in society, whether during the Renaissance or in the new millennium, as being consigned to the position of possession. Men, by contrast, are in positions of power capable of possessing women, whether they possess women physically or by simply owning the gaze. According to these scholars, the success of our lives is based on how we appear to others. In my former partner's eyes, I was unacceptable. I was thus unsuccessful, a failure – in life and as a woman.

Media studies scholars articulate the various ways images of women can affect our self-esteem and our self-image. Objectification theory and social comparison theory acknowledge the role of media in this process but go further by incorporating psychological theory to elucidate the way these messages and the resulting thoughts and behaviors manifest.

Objectification theory posits that when women learn – through cultural messages and lived experiences – to see themselves as sexual objects or objects of desire, we learn to view ourselves and our bodies as objects and to evaluate our bodies and ourselves in terms of whether or not we are pleasing to others. A basic tenet of objectification theory is that dominant cultural messages about gender and appearance, which I contend largely emanate from the various forms of media we consume, can promote self-objectification.

Recently, scholars have begun to argue that objectification theory does not influence self-esteem unilaterally, but rather in conjunction with other psychological theories such as social comparison theory, that more effectively identify the very real consequences of sexual objectification. The central premise of social comparison theory is that we generally have a desire or a tendency to evaluate ourselves and to compare ourselves with others, and these comparisons can provide relevant information about appearance, weight, desirability, and so on. For American women who are routinely subjected to images of an impossible ideal, these comparisons can negatively affect our self-perception. My failure to be a Victoria's Secret model meant I was not only a failure as a woman, but that I should be ashamed of myself and my body as a result. And I was.

The sexual objectification of women and cultural messages about appearance encourage us to focus on our appearance above all else, believing that only when we fit the cultural standard of tall, leggy, skinny, large-breasted, and beautiful will we be successful, desirable, and happy. The problem is that women not only internalize these messages, but so do our significant others (or potential significant others).

Women are continually reminded, both by media and by those with whom we interact, to constantly monitor and evaluate our bodies against the American ideal. While men evaluate our bodies, we also evaluate other women as a form of social comparison to determine our social desirability. Women are not only objectified, we self-objectify as we compare ourselves against the American ideal and against other women. We monitor ourselves to determine whether or not we meet societal standards of desirability, beauty, and appearance in order to gauge our success and happiness.

I realized that my body had changed, although I was a size 4. My son had been born a few years earlier and my body was different. I was no longer a perfect 34, but I looked pretty damned good for someone with a four-year-old son. Still, I was compared to Victoria's Secret models. I have realized over the years that my former partner was simply a victim of the culture in which he lives, as most of us are. As Berger argued, women are portrayed differently from men because the "ideal" spectator is always assumed to be a man and the woman is displayed as his object of desire. He wasn't being malicious, though it felt like it at the time. He was simply reiterating what so many others before him had declared: there is an ideal and women should strive to achieve it.

The American Psychological Association recognizes the pervasive objectification of women in the United States and points to the media's practice of fragmenting women's bodies, something Sut Jhally also highlights in *Dreamworlds 3*, as responsible not only for the dehumanization of women but for the increased likelihood of violence against us. A recent study of partner-objectification reported that while women tend to be more inclined toward body shame than men, men tend to focus more on their romantic partner's appearance and criticize it (Sanchez, Good, Kwang, & Eric Saltzman, 2008). The study revealed that the more frequently men expressed concerns about their partner's appearance (size, weight, clothing, wrinkles, etc.), the less satisfaction they reported in their relationship. A similar study suggests this is the result of seeing one's partner as an object of sexual pleasure rather than as a thinking, feeling person (Zurbriggen, Ramsey, & Jaworski, 2011). In his eyes, I was little more than a sexual object, not a breathing woman with a child.

He did not abuse me physically, though I had suffered intense physical abuse from my father and from the first man with whom I ever had a relationship). I suffered emotional abuse from them as well, and my father was the king of psychological abuse. Unfortunately, as a young child, I learned I would never be good enough, smart enough, pretty enough, tall enough, or anything enough.

I resolved never to let another man lay a hand on me, and no man has since that time. The emotional and psychological abuse, however, continued unabated. My ex-husband was a monster and routinely told me I was lucky to have him and that without him I would never amount to anything. (Should I mention that he couldn't get accepted to an MBA program, but I earned my Ph.D. from one of the top-ranked programs in the country? After we were divorced, of course.) But this man, the one who wanted me to be a Victoria's Secret model, engaged in a different type of emotional and psychological abuse.

He never told me I was beautiful. Ever. He routinely criticized my appearance, even though I had lost all my baby weight and was down to a size 4 within a year of my son's birth. He told me I was fat and that I needed to exercise, to work out, to dress differently, to do whatever it was he deemed necessary for me to meet the cultural ideal he believed was so important. He took control of my identity and convinced me I was unattractive, fat, and undesirable. When we occasionally split up (we were together for nearly four years), he would immediately throw temper tantrums to my friends and complain about how I "dressed up" when we weren't together, but not when we were together. My friends would explain that I dressed no differently, he simply saw me differently. I always took him back, mostly because I thought I'd never find anyone else. He succeeded in convincing me of that. I bought into the belief that I needed a man to be happy or successful as a woman and he preyed on that belief. But the day he opened the Victoria's Secret catalog and demanded I look and dress like them was the day something inside me clicked, the day something changed. I had already been accepted to several doctoral programs and had made my choice. He told me I shouldn't go because I would fail. Perhaps that last bit of condemnation was the impetus I needed to succeed on my own terms, without anybody, in record time, and with accolades. Perhaps I succeeded just to spite him. Maybe I had it inside me all along. But it took nearly three decades of objectification and abuse for me to realize my own potential.

It has taken me years to acknowledge the normalization that is objectification. It has taken me years to unlearn self-objectification. I admit I'm guilty of social comparison. Sometimes it doesn't affect me, but other times it does. I still often believe I'm not beautiful enough or smart enough or successful enough, especially in comparison to others. But I realize I'm not a twenty-something anymore, so the standards of beauty for me should be different, even if they aren't (just look at Goldie Hawn and others – lambasted by media at a recent Academy Awards – who rely on cosmetic surgery to maintain an ideal that is utterly unrealistic). Much of my awakening is the result of my post-graduate education and subsequent research and scholarship, as well as the years I have spent teaching and realizing that students truly don't recognize the many subtle ways media influences them.

I have always questioned the images I see in media. I questioned the images of Brooke Shields donning her Calvin Klein jeans. Truth be told, they were so skin tight, nothing could have come between her and those jeans. I questioned why June Cleaver cleaned house in a dress, heels, and pearls. My mom never cleaned house looking like that, and why would she? Housework is messy business.

When I neared the end of my master's program, I found a method for critically analyzing the media images I saw, an approach I refined during my doctoral program. I have spent my academic career critically analyzing media images to identify the messages they send, most of which are unconscious and normalized. No matter what course I teach, I incorporate critical media analysis. I have discovered that, despite being surrounded by media, most people aren't media literate and are thus easily manipulated by it. It is my mission in life to minimize the media's influence on my students. We compare and contrast images of women and men in the media: the absurdly thin, waiflike women and the beautifully muscular men. We talk about how sexualized men's bodies are very different from sexualized women's bodies because in order to be supremely muscular, men must eat healthily and exercise. In order for women to look the way our media counterparts do, they must be born into the two percent of women on Earth who are naturally tall and thin without a hint of body fat (meaning they can't have boobs, so if they do, they're fake because boobs are fatty – or adipose – tissue), or they suffer from disordered eating or drug abuse (or both). The images and the standards are very different.

I rub the screen every time I have an image up of one of those male models or athletes with the beautiful six-pack abs. I really want to feel abs like that. I'm not sure they're real, or that they really exist. But I'd love to feel them. My students always laugh at me. I'm human, I tell them. Sure, I love looking at the images, but then we talk about the reality, about what these people look like in real life. I tell them about the young female student I had when I was a graduate teaching assistant. She was a model. That's how she paid her way through school. Her photos were spectacularly beautiful. She talked to me about how tired she was of people telling her she was too thin, that she needed to eat more. She said she wore the biggest, baggiest clothes she could find so people couldn't see how thin she was. Her eyes always had dark circles under them, her cheeks seemed to sink into her face. She said it was the only way she could afford college because her parents couldn't help her. She looked like hell, actually. Heroin-chic to the extreme. But her modeling photos were phenomenal.

I think about Marilyn Monroe. In her day, she was considered the most beautiful woman on Earth. I'll never forget the day when some students walked into my office, and upon seeing one of my posters of Marilyn on the wall, one said, "Oh my God! She's so fat! If I looked like her I'd kill myself!" I just stared at her. I couldn't even talk. It was the first time in my life I ever remember being truly speechless. Literally. I honestly didn't know what to say.

The next day in class I asked my students if I was fat. The room was dead silent. Nobody would even look at me. "I'm serious," I said. "I want your honest opinion." One of my students said, "You're a MILF." The class erupted in laughter. Well, mostly the guys laughed. The ladies were a bit uncomfortable. "I've been told that before," I said. "But seriously, do you think I'm fat?" The general consensus was that I was not fat. I was healthy, athletic, muscular. Most students admired me because I'm an avid rock climber. And I don't look my age. At all. It's another strike against me, actually, because men think I'm younger, and when they find out how old I really am, they run, screaming, far, far away.

At the time, I actually was fat. For me. I was between a size 10 and a 12. That's normal for women. But normal for me has always been a size 6. Regardless, my students said I wasn't fat. At the time, I was the same size Marilyn Monroe had been at the height of her fame and popularity. I told my students this, and showed several images of her. I then showed some images of me and, admittedly, in the photos I looked heavier. I explained that the camera adds five to ten pounds. So Marilyn Monroe was actually not fat. Neither was I. Consider, then, what Victoria's Secret models really look like. "If you can see their bones in these pictures, imagine what they look like in real life," I told my students. They were silent. I then showed Jean Kilbourne's (2000) *Killing Us Softly 3: Advertising's Images of Women.* You could have heard a pin drop. And the rooms were carpeted. That says something.

I am a feminist. I am a scholar. I am a woman who appreciates and embraces who and how she is. And I thank the many scholars who have come before me to elucidate the means and methods society uses to perpetuate a particular status quo, one that is inherently patriarchal, but one into which women have achieved great inroads. I love my son, who I raised to be a feminist (he often makes comments that make me want to punch him in the throat; he does it just to see my reaction so he can laugh at me). I love men. After more than thirteen years single and celibate (not by choice, trust me), I am in a happy and fulfilling relationship with a man who respects me for who and how I am, who thinks I am beautiful and tells me so every day, and who is turned on by my intelligence. Should I mention that he is significantly younger than me? Cougars be damned.

I'm not a Victoria's Secret model. I never have been and I never will be. I am me. Curvy, voluptuous, me. I'm no longer a perfect 34, but I'm pretty perfect, especially for someone my age. And I've discovered that even though men my age don't want me, younger men do. I believe it was Rita Rudner who said, "Women hit their sexual peak in their forties and men hit their sexual peak in their twenties. What kind of cruel joke is that?" It's kind of fun, though, to be aging so gracefully and to be perfectly satisfied with who and how I am. Well, mostly satisfied. I'm not sure a day goes by that I don't wish I was an inch taller. So I compromise: I wear heels.

DISCUSSION QUESTIONS

1. What do you consider to be the ideal woman? How did you develop this image?

2. Do an online search for some of the classical nudes from the Renaissance (e.g., Ingres' *Grand Odalisque* or Manet's *Le Dejeuner sur l'Herbe*). Then do a search for contemporary fashion advertisements. Compare the images. What do these images say about women and how women should look, act, and dress?

3. Visit MediaEd.org and watch the trailers for *Killing Us Softly 4, Dreamworlds 3,* and *The Codes of Gender.* Do you think the way you look at yourself – and how others look at you – has been shaped by the media? Do you look at yourself any differently now?

REFERENCES

Berger, J. (1972). *Ways of seeing.* London: British Broadcasting Corporation.

Media Education Foundation. (Producer), & Jhally, S. (Director). (1997). *Dreamworlds II: Desire, sex, power in music video* [DVD]. Available from http://www.mediaed.org

Media Education Foundation. (Producer), & Jhally, S. (Director). (2010). *Dreamworlds 3: Desire, sex, & power in music video* [DVD]. Available from http://www.mediaed.org

Media Education Foundation. (Producer), & Kilbourne, J., & Jhally, S. (Directors). (2000). *Killing us softly 3: Advertising's images of women* [DVD].

Sanchez, D. T., Good, J. J., Kwang, T., & Saltzman, E. (2008). When finding a mate feels urgent: Why relationship contingency predicts men's and women's body shame. *Social Psychology, 39,* 90–102.

Scott, J. (2011). *The other side of life.* Bangor, ME: jessINK.

Simonton, A. J. (1995). Women for sale. In C. M. Lont (Ed.), *Women and media: Content, careers, criticism* (pp. 143–164). Belmont, CA: Wadsworth.

Zurbriggen, E. L., Ramsey, L. R., & Jaworski, B. K. (2011). Self- and partner-objectification in romantic relationships: Associations with media consumption and relationship satisfaction. *Sex Roles, 64,* 452.

JEAN KILBOURNE

17. THE EPHEMERAL PASSPORT

I have benefitted from many unearned privileges in my life. I was born into a middle-class white family in the United States, thereby winning several spins of the roulette wheel. While I may have missed out on male privilege, I didn't face being judged negatively by my skin color or my class. I didn't have to beg for food. I wasn't denied an education or forced to marry a much older man. And I didn't have to swim across the Rio Grande or traverse the Aegean Sea in search of a better life.

There is increasing awareness of many of these privileges. This essay is about a privilege that is almost taboo to mention – the privilege of beauty. Books have been written about beauty, of course, and it has been the subject of some of my own academic work. But this piece is not a treatise, not a scholarly work. It is a personal reflection on how the unearned privilege of beauty has affected my life.

I was born to exceptionally good-looking parents. My mother did some modeling before she married. My father had the dark, handsome looks of a movie star like Gregory Peck or Tyrone Power. I once introduced a friend to him, adding, "Handsome, isn't he?" My mother told me later, quite sharply, never to say that again. So I learned there was something unseemly, perhaps even embarrassing, about being aware of physical beauty – and certainly it was not to be mentioned.

My mother died of cancer when she was forty-one and I was nine. Throughout my life this has been, in the words of the poet César Vallejo, "my silver wound, my eternal loss". I watched my mother lose her beauty and then her life within a few months. No one told my three brothers and me what was happening, and people rarely spoke of her afterwards. For several years after that I felt invisible – in my family, at school, in the world. My brothers and I were each in our own private prisons of repressed grief. Sometimes I sat in my mother's empty closet, just to be close to her scent.

My father, a hero who fought on the front lines in WWII, suffered from unrecognized PTSD, as did so many of those brave men. Often away on business, he was ill-equipped to raise four children on his own. He did the

P. Leavy (Ed.), Privilege Through the Looking-Glass, 125–130.

best he could, but my childhood was bleak and sad. I suffered from recurring bouts of depression for many years.

After my mother died, I lost almost all my friends. Other children didn't know how to talk to me and neither did their parents. Maybe they feared such loss and grief were contagious. I used to say that I was a freak, but freaks are stared at and I was unseen. I had been a popular little girl but I quickly became a lonely one. My companions were my books and my pet guinea pig.

One of the few memories I have of the years immediately following my mother's death is that I liked to pretend I was walking on the ceilings of my home. I would look into a hand mirror as I walked through the house, carefully stepping over thresholds and walking around light fixtures. Indeed, my world was as upside down and empty as those ceilings. I began having a nightmare that was to persist for decades. In this dream, I am buried alive. I can hear people walking on my grave but when I open my mouth to scream for help, I am suddenly mute.

I used to fantasize that I would find a magic potion that would make people notice me, maybe even love me – some lucky charm that would make me the center of attention. Suddenly, when I was sixteen, my fantasy came true. Seemingly overnight I was deemed beautiful and I became highly visible, especially to men. I first realized this when, to my complete astonishment, I won a beauty contest in my hometown, a contest I had entered on a dare.

From the very beginning, even though I had longed for it, I felt extremely ambivalent about this gift. Being stared at made me nervous, made me feel that something was terribly wrong. The spotlight that focused on me in mid-adolescence was shocking, scary, seductive, compelling. Having "won the lottery," I went from poverty to riches in less than a year. I never felt that it had anything to do with me.

At the same time, I knew beauty had extraordinary value and that the dread of losing it was the ever-present dark side. As in the old fairy tales, every gift comes with a price, a curse. I was particularly haunted by the fear that any man I loved would eventually leave me for someone young when I grew old. Whatever the reason, I was aware from the very beginning that my looks were not simply a blessing. It was probably this realization more than any other that eventually led to my work of challenging and deconstructing the beauty myth.

I was no Sophia Loren or Elizabeth Taylor, but for many years a day seldom went by without someone commenting on my appearance. I rarely found myself beautiful, although sometimes I thought I might be if I were carefully groomed and polished and the light was just right. Always aware of every flaw, I felt a terrible gap between the way the world perceived me and the way I felt about myself.

Upon my graduation from Wellesley College, I had to go to secretarial school to get a job. Options for women were extremely limited in the early 1960s. People encouraged me to model, which was one of the few ways a woman could make a lot of money. My brief forays into modeling were seductive but soul-destroying, and played a big role in my lifelong interest in the power of the image.

One day I went to New York and modeled for a world-famous fashion designer. I'd never been on a runway before and I barely knew how to move. After the show, the designer invited me back to his home, where he told me that I could have a successful and lucrative career as a model. All I had to do was sleep with him. I went back to Boston and to my eighty-dollar-a-week job as a waitress. My depression deepened.

Through a newspaper ad, I got a job doing some ghostwriting for Al Capp. He was a smart and witty man, but bitter and cynical. He liked my writing very much. He also wanted sex in exchange for the job. His manager called me and said, "Go to bed with him, honey – it won't kill you". I thought it might, but I was desperate. I loved the intellectual challenge of the work I was doing with Capp and was bored with every other job I had ever had. I was also broke.

This was one of the lowest points of my life. I could rationalize that the fashion designer wouldn't hire me unless I slept with him. After all, I thought, modeling is a form of selling one's body anyway. But Capp thought I was brilliant. He thought I could write. But that wasn't enough. I was still going to have to put my body on the line.

After turning Capp down, I had a series of mindless jobs. One of them was placing ads into *The Lancet*, a medical journal. And one of these ads changed my life. It was a typical ad – insulting to women, demeaning. Yet at that moment it somehow crystallized so many of my experiences: the sexist slights, the terrible jobs, the catcalls, the objectification. I thought, "This is atrocious, and it is not trivial". I began collecting ads and putting them on my refrigerator with magnets, gradually seeing patterns and themes. I created a slide presentation which eventually became my first film, *Killing Us Softly: Advertising's Image of Women*, which I made in 1979 (and have remade three times since).

I traveled all around the country, giving more than a hundred lectures a year, mostly on college campuses. People often commented on my appearance – sometimes judging me to be too much like the models in my presentation, as if feminists could present themselves in only one stereotypical way. I knew that someday, as I grew older, the tables might turn and some people would say that my critique of the image was simply sour grapes. Feminists can't win the beauty game. Gloria Steinem was faulted for being too beautiful, Betty Friedan for being "unattractive".

Pointing out the downside of being beautiful is a lot like complaining about being rich or famous. Oh please. But beauty is unlike most other forms of privilege because it is transient, short-lived, especially for women. A man said to me once, "Your beauty is an international passport".

"Maybe," I replied, "but one day it will be revoked". I often thought that being a beautiful young woman was like being very rich but with the absolute knowledge that someday one would be bankrupt. Beautiful celebrities are shamed for aging, and shamed for attempting to erase the signs of aging. At the end of beauty is contempt, hostility, and invisibility.

I have to admit that I sometimes enjoyed and capitalized on the sense of power that beauty creates. Looking back, I sometimes wish I had enjoyed it more. But the power is mostly illusory. I was hired for virtually every job I ever sought – but that didn't help me succeed or keep the job. I was sexually harassed during most of them. I was often stopped for speeding but never got a ticket. When I entered a party, I was never alone for long. Beautiful women are magnets for narcissistic men and the adulation such men initially shower on women can feel like love…but it isn't.

Beautiful young women learn early on that many men want to have sex with them. Married men, men of all ages. This can easily lead to contempt for men. So many men who were with other women came on to me that I began to wonder if faithful and monogamous men existed. Many are so easily distracted by a shiny new object.

To be beautiful is to be an object and the constant objectification can be frightening and exhausting. Contempt is the flip side of the adoration of the sex symbol. I remember sunbathing on the banks of the Charles River in Cambridge one afternoon. Some men came by in a boat quite close to shore. They shouted and whistled at me and wouldn't leave me alone. Eventually I got up to leave and shot them the finger. The rage came off the boat like a wake, and their shouts of "bitch" and "whore" followed me all the way to the street.

Another high price of beauty is that it can alienate other women. Fear of this has made me reluctant to write this essay, even though I am writing about the past. Many years ago, I reconnected with a friend from elementary school. I expressed joy that we could be friends again and she replied she could never be friends with someone so beautiful. "I would feel erased every time I stood beside you," she said. This made me so sad. Sometimes other women misinterpreted my essential shyness as aloofness, vanity. Fortunately, many women did not feel this way and I have been blessed with very deep friendships, relationships that have sustained me throughout my life.

Perhaps the highest price is the knowledge that all this power will one day be gone. I was ambivalent about it but I also counted on it, was used to it. I remember reading a passage in Doris Lessing's *The Summer Before the Dark* in which the protagonist walks past some construction workers and is unnoticed. As I recall, she removes her coat and walks by again and gets sexual comments and whistles. She knows she is on the edge of invisibility. I was in my twenties when I read it, and I shuddered. I knew this inevitably would be my fate too.

I had become visible almost overnight. The invisibility came much more slowly. For quite some time I could turn the visibility back on, with my clothes or makeup or even just by the way I walked. But those days are long gone. Now people walk through me on the sidewalk. I have to ask for help putting my luggage in the overhead bin on a plane. I enter a party and look for other women to talk with (I always did this but men would circle in and they no longer do).

I can't say that becoming invisible is painless, but it has surprised me that it is much less painful than I expected. There is some relief and a great deal of privacy in no longer being a sex object. An old friend, known more for her candor than her tact, said to me not long ago that she was finding it hard to have "lost her looks". "But I was only pretty," she said. "You were a great beauty – it must be terrible for you". I had to laugh because it was such an outrageous thing to say, and yet so honest.

Perhaps it is not so terrible because I've had a lot of time to adjust to it. Perhaps it's not so terrible because I had a career that didn't depend on my looks (although my looks were not irrelevant). Most likely it's not so terrible because I am happy in my life. I'm blessed with an amazing daughter, excellent friends, a sweet dog, and work that I love. I've made enough money that I can live comfortably and travel from time to time. Most important, I am visible to the people who love me and I no longer crave the attention of strangers.

I do resent that men don't go through this. A man my age and in my general state of health and fitness would still be considered sexy and desirable, especially if he had money and authority. He could command attention. The pool of possible partners for men widens as they age whereas it shrinks to a dewdrop for women. Success makes men more desirable and more likely to find a partner. The opposite is true for women.

Sometimes I miss my passport. But more often I realize that it took me to lands I didn't really want to visit, places that were alien to my true self. Today I choose my traveling companions more wisely. And I feel more at home in my body – my aging, imperfect body – and my life than ever before.

DISCUSSION QUESTIONS

1. What role has your appearance played in your life?
2. Have you ever felt invisible? If so, how?
3. Do you think people get unfair benefits due to their looks? Explain your response.
4. What do you think advertising tells us about female beauty?

LISA PHILLIPS

18. IT'S A SMALL WORLD

The Metabletics of Size

The support group is scheduled to begin in a few minutes. Mostly women, and a few men are milling about. Some are staring into their Styrofoam cups of coffee or tea. Chairs are arranged in a circle, and when the meeting comes to order, a few folks choose to sit behind the circle that has been arranged. They look less physically exposed and perhaps less vulnerable from that position. After introductions are made and the group process reviewed, the first person speaks. "I grew up with 16 aunts and uncles and they were all ashamed to be related to me because I was so fat. When I was just five years old, my mother's meanest sister, Val, told me that she and her husband, Uncle Mick, would love me and buy me a new dress if I would just lose weight. As if I were the boss and making my own food! Even at that young age, I knew that something was more wrong with those adults than with me; over the years, however, I weakened and started to believe it was me that was wrong, flawed, and insane about food and everything else". Heads can be seen nodding and others begin to take their turn sharing.

"I was a failure-to-thrive baby. Can you believe it? Just wouldn't eat when I was born! My father died in battle just a few weeks later, and I didn't even have a name. He only got to hold me once or twice. My mother was wrecked by his death and couldn't help but wreck me, I guess. I heard a fancy doctor talk about childhood trauma once, and since I had a number of them, I was really interested. He said that for kids like me, the brain went from zero to sixty at the first tiny sign of distress, and that it was not wired like normal, like it was supposed to be, leaving me without things he called 'self-soothing skills and proper emotional regulation.' Maybe that's why I'm hungry all the time too".

"My buddies and I were at our Catholic junior high school activity day at an amusement park. We couldn't wait to ride the daring rides. It was an old, sort of run-down place, but it was famous for its wooden rollercoasters. The lines were fairly long, and in order to get up on the platform of the

P. Leavy (Ed.), Privilege Through the Looking-Glass, 131–141.

main coaster, you had to line up next to the side of the building in a narrow ascending row with a metal bannister, opposite the wall, to hold onto as you climbed closer to the top. When I finally got to the front of the line, my friend Tony quickly pushed through the old-fashioned metal turnstile that led to the platform. I was next. I got stuck in the turnstile. It wouldn't budge. I was too big. I had to physically hurt myself to step back out of it. The ride operator tried to cover for me. He told me to go ahead and walk up the exit ramp to get onto the platform that way. But in order to do that, I had to first walk back down that narrow ramp next to the building where people were lined up and waiting. It was a walk of shame and humiliation where I was laughed at and called every name in the book. "He can't fit!" roared from person to person down the line. I made my way back down that ramp through all those people throwing word grenades, never looking anyone in the eye, trying to keep a stiff upper lip. I never rode a single ride that day, or ever since".

These are just a few of the stark memories of people who deal with morbid and profound obesity, often with childhood onset. I know them as some of the bravest souls to walk the planet because for many, just leaving their homes in the morning and going to work can be an assaultive experience. Fat shaming is a *thing* now. No one is exempt, from celebrities to the unsuspecting Walmart shoppers who may not look their best some days. While people often stop at nearby coffee shops for a beverage and breakfast on their way to work, for the person carrying a significant amount of weight, their order oftentimes comes with free 'side' of hurt. Reading people's aversive body language and enduring subtle and not-so-subtle looks of disdain is often accompanied by overhearing, for example, some of the following: how the "super-sized girl" will be holding up the line because of the big order she will most likely place; how that guy should grab three tickets for all the space he takes up in line; how you should not touch the counter because the sweaty fatty slimed it all up; and how awesome it was to see the daily-race-to-diabetes kickoff for the "Gigantor or Metabolic Molly" first thing in the morning.

The impulse to speak negatively to and about overweight individuals painfully knows no bounds. Professionals and leaders who have devoted their lives to the healing arts, helping countless people, are not immune to this lapse into fat bashing. What follows are a just a few of many examples to illustrate some of the adverse effects. A profoundly obese woman once shared with me that she was excited to start taking better care of herself in small steps, starting with a vitamin regimen. On the first day of her new self-care plan, she was watching a PBS special where a man who wrote a famous health and fitness book was doing a question-and-answer series. When asked by an audience member about the benefits of taking vitamins, he answered the person, who was only slightly plump, that he would not give vitamins to a pig because it would be like throwing them in a garbage dump. So what sense, he reasoned, would it make for an overweight person to take them? The woman viewing the program was upset and truly believed it was no accident that she was watching. For her, it was a sign that she was on the wrong path yet again.

A distinguished, well-respected psychologist and author, in a seminal training book for graduate students, derided fat children from his youth and provided merciless examples of how to handle fat adults who enter treatment. When this disparaging content was questioned by several graduate students, the professor who taught the course and had selected the textbook for study stated that if people were looking to be offended, they could find just about any example to meet their needs. Feeling embarrassed and unheard, the sensitive students just let the matter drop. Though it was nearly a decade later in the telling, the story still upset the person who recently recounted it to me. He felt like he should have done more to put a stop to the use of that loathsome material.

A local pastor who has long struggled with his weight shared that his morning routine includes stretches while he watches a global ministry show on TV that his church is affiliated with, and to which it provides ongoing financial support. On one particular program, the renowned minister featured a religious medical doctor who had written a book on diet and exercise. The minister bragged that he had followed this doctor's advice and lost 50 pounds. He was encouraging all the "fat darlings" in the church to get off their butts and to stop eating themselves to death, assuring them that they would look and feel so much better. He chided them to not get mad at him for saying that, because he was doing so only "in love." The medical doctor chimed in that people ought to know how great life is without the burden of excess weight, and after all, gluttony is a sin! He then explained that while he and his wife were flying in to tape the television show, they had a "horrible" experience with a woman in their airplane row who was "so huge" that she not only spilled over into the next seat, making another passenger visibly uncomfortable, but she also had to have a special seat belt extender because she was the size of two or three people. For the pastor who was watching, the implication was that the woman had no idea what a disgusting imposition she was to the world. He shared with me that he felt as if he took a punch to his solar plexus after listening to all the comments that were made on the program that day.

Heartrending stories equally abound from patients of family physicians, gynecologists, and endocrinologists, to name a few, whose important health-related feedback may include a dose of cruelty and contempt. A gentleman I recently encountered informed me that his family physician and his pulmonologist both fired him because he could not lose weight or follow the plan of eating they had established for him. He was told that they could not help him, that he was only getting worse, and that he should try to find physicians who could "deal" with him. He described being made to feel like a total, hopeless moral degenerate because of his inability to successfully lose weight.

Though adults struggle mightily with the issues that accompany obesity, it is vulnerable overweight children in our society who must endure years of life-altering ridicule, toxic shaming, and debilitating exclusion and isolation. In some instances, by the time children are of school age, their size and eating habits have already become "their own faults". Kindergarteners are told to stop making pigs of themselves and to leave something for the other kids when they take a cookie or milk with lunch like their normal-weight peers. In other cases, parents have been told by school and healthcare authorities that the severity of their child's obesity could result in a report to Child Protective Services, with the threat of having their child removed. Whether the child, the parent, or both are being blamed, this approach has been of little assistance to families. In observing antibullying groups for children and adolescents, one of the most targeted subsets that are represented are kids who are overweight. Even within the group itself, safeguards have to be put in place to keep the normal-weight children from picking on or shunning their larger peers. Parents of group members have shared that they are mortified to hear their own children, who were bullied firsthand, say that they don't like a certain person in the group because he or she has fat legs, or that the fat kids should be in their own antibullying group because they are ugly and gross.

Researchers began studying size-discrimination among children in 1961. In one replicated study, reported in *Obesity Research* in November of 2003, a major increase (over 40%) in bias toward overweight children was found. Given the choice of six drawings, children were still least likely to pick the heavier child to be their friend, preferring drawings that included a child in a wheelchair or with facial disfigurement. Any psychotherapist who is working with an overweight child, or an adult who once was an obese child, can speak to the effects of stigma, social isolation, suicidal thoughts, body- and self-hatred, and the self-blame that often result from peer, and at times educator, rejection. Campaigns to promote diversity in size, and overall size acceptance among children, have led to some school districts balking, citing the "war on obesity" and "not being willing to contribute to the obesity epidemic." One parent shared with me that her local school district was confronting the issue of obesity by disgracing the parents and their overweight children. When this mother tried to address the fact that her son could not easily fit into classroom chairs with attached desktops, no special accommodations were made. The school administration declared that they had no intention of enabling their students to remain so overweight and unhealthy. Since summer was coming, they recommended the student "do something about his weight before the start of [the] next year".

For children and adolescents, social media continues to be a modern-day culprit, where they are belittled for any number of reasons, not the least of which is for being obese. Tragic reports of preteen and teen suicide abound and are widely covered in the media. Still, in communities all around this country, the lack of peer acceptance and the resulting brutalities persist. Horror stories of the overweight adolescent girl who is asked to a formal dance or prom as a joke still continue. A beautifully attired obese teen waiting for her date, who never arrives to take her to the event, is not just a tragic scene from a movie. One girl in an antibullying group related how this actually happened to her a year ago. She recounted that when her date no-showed, her grandfather put on an old suit and drove her into the city for an expensive dinner. Despite his attempt to console her, she could not stop crying that night, or for days on end. When the school district was alerted about the situation, no formal disciplinary action ensued for those who were involved. As a result of what occurred, the girl refused to go back to her district and is now attending cyberschool. In addition, prior to the big night, she disclosed having to struggle through countless microaggressions (i.e., indirect, subtle, or unintentional discrimination against members of a marginalized group). When she and her mother went to look for dress ideas, several sales associates at different stores quickly assessed her body and said, "we don't carry plus-sizes, or big sizes, or anything that would fit you". When she was getting her hair swept up for the big night at a salon, the stylist said, "Your date must be a real special kid; they didn't have guys who overlooked stuff like that when I was in school," referring to the teen's larger size.

Adolescents who struggle with their weight often share in the antibullying groups how ashamed they feel when they have to eat in public, be it in the school cafeteria or at a restaurant with their families. One young man revealed that he has not eaten lunch at school for over three years due to the taunting that occurred no matter what he ate, including salads. Another adolescent girl shared that when she is out with her family on their weekly pizza night, she has heard normal-weight peers at nearby tables loudly remark that they had better not eat anything because they are too fat, then look at her and giggle. On one occasion, a waitress even leaned over, handed her a giant stack of napkins, and whispered that they were for her to blot the excess oil from her pizza.

Many overweight teens prefer to avoid extracurricular activities and public events or places due to the threat of verbal abuse at every turn, especially during the summer months. Spending time at a public pool or the beach is equated with the threat of becoming the next viral video. Shouts of "beached whale walking" or "human manatee" accompany posted cell phone videos of unsuspecting people of size. As a result, this has greatly limited the willingness of many obese adolescents to be even seen in public.

Teens also describe an unlimited litany of insensitive questions that they are frequently asked by adults and peers. How can you go walking every day and still be that overweight? How can you be a vegan and still be so fat? Were you this size when you and your boyfriend started dating? Are you some kind of big football jock or something, is that how you got a girl to like you? Did you have some kind of psycho childhood that made you so fat? Did your parents not love you or did they neglect you or something? Did you have a Chester the Molester in your family that made you like this? Why are you the only fat one in your family? These difficult and demeaning scenarios continue as teens move into their college years. More than one overweight student has had his or her roommate request a reassignment because of a reaction to living with a "fat freak," "an ugly fat mess," or "a lazy dirty pig." One obese student shared overhearing her roommate say she was "a total fat loser," "an embarrassment," and "not even good enough to be a decent DUFF [designated ugly fat friend]". Her roommate blamed this overweight teen for ruining her chances to date cute guys on campus. As if situations like this are not discouraging enough, college students who are obese have often been denied entrance to social and even service organizations. Their intelligence, talents, commitment, and work ethic have been dramatically underestimated. They have also been denied campus leadership positions because they may be too "lazy" to do all the work required, and because no one would want to join an organization that had an obese person at the helm.

Exposure to size prejudice arises not only from others, but also from the structural world itself. Booths of all manner, tall tables with high stools, concert venues, stadiums, school bleachers without railings, outdoor furniture, old movie theaters, nearly full elevators, chairs with arms, airline seats, compact and larger cars with low steering wheels, and recreational activities like haunted houses, carriage or hot-air-balloon rides, horseback riding, parasailing, and riding the rapids are just part of the everyday, and recreational, obstacle course that presents potential hazards for a person of size. For morbidly and profoundly obese individuals, the lived world of shared public space is small, stressful, and unsafe. As a result, every new experience is not something to look forward to, but something to dread, to be vigilant or hypervigilant about, and if possible, to check out ahead of time. For the older obese person with some physical limitations, there are even more considerations. Is there on-street parking? How far will I need to walk? Are there a ton of steps? Do they only have an outdoor patio open for lunch that faces the sidewalk? Is the seating sturdy and made of wood? What are the busiest hours, so I can avoid people? Should I have someone do a dry-run for me to check out the place first? Where is the best place to sit to be near the bathrooms and close to the door as well? What will require the least amount of walking? Unlike their normal-weight counterparts, who would consider finding a plum parking spot or obtaining preferred seating merely a boon (with every location and seat being an option for them), for the person of size, it is all a carefully choreographed dance geared toward whether they can even make it into an establishment, find seating that can accommodate them, and do so without exacerbated physical impairment or profound embarrassment along the way. Their choices are, unfortunately, are always limited.

For as many obese people as there are with physical impairments using seated scooters in grocery and department stores, there are even more who are too impaired or mortified to leave their homes, much less bear being a "riding target". The overt humiliation and shunning that can occur when a person carrying a significant amount of weight does bravely enter the outside world and is finally settled into a given small space is often instantaneous, rarely subtle, and explains, in part, why obese people often hide. Frequently, people around the large person will move their seats, turn their faces, and if possible, their backs. If a pleasantry is finally exchanged with a normal-weight person, it can range from an immensely awkward encounter to an intensely stiff politeness that quickly dismisses and closes the door to future interaction. This, however, pales in comparison to the stunning rejection that can only be leveled by another person of size. A large beautiful woman once shared with me that she liked to surround herself with thin people because they were better accepted, had more friends, and enabled her to be less self-conscious and to live vicariously through them. Perhaps that explains some of blatant intolerance that obese people report experiencing from other people of size.

More recently in the media, plus-sized body activists who are models and photographers are taking a beating, but nevertheless are out in the world and no longer hiding themselves. These courageous women and men are not encouraging obesity or trying to deny its associated health risks; what they are denying is the limits imposed on their freedom to make improvements to their lives and health, *or not*, just like every other respectable citizen of the world. The accusation that these public figures are trying to normalize obesity may be well-founded, if normalizing means recognizing that obese people are a valuable part, and an expression of, the human family. The world has likely been populated by people of different shapes and sizes from the beginning of time. The current Western diet certainly cannot be cited as influencing the amazing works of art from the Renaissance that depict large, gorgeous women. Those artists were not accused of encouraging obesity, but were rather lauded for capturing women in the fullness and truth of their lived bodies. Perhaps a better way for normal-weight individuals to view these current trailblazing people of size is to see the barriers they are breaking through as necessary steps to encourage awareness, understanding, respect, and perhaps, most importantly, acceptance toward people with diverse bodies. In so doing, people of size will have more freedom to be accepting and unashamed of themselves as they reach toward their goals and levels of emotional wellbeing and health.

One additional area of size prejudice that bears mentioning targets professional people of size. Studies indicate that physical fitness and health consciousness are associated with higher levels of education. Doctors, teachers, and business professionals with more lucrative salaries are less likely to be obese; less-educated individuals with poorly paying jobs are more likely to be obese. Despite these findings, highly educated, successful, well-paid human beings can still be persons of considerable size. And when they are, the discrimination sometimes levied at them can be more deeply personal. Many overweight successful professionals report being accused of being overly aggressive, fierce, intense, overpowering, and downright scary. If they possess a powerful intellect, the aforementioned perceptions are even more heightened, and they are found to be "doubly intimidating". Normal-weight professional peers with comparable personality styles and talents are rarely labeled with similar terms. A student in medical school described this as the law of the jungle: the bigger the animal, the deadlier the threat. One obese professional shared that since he could not immediately become smaller in size, he had to accommodate others by becoming smaller in authority, knowledge, and power. A female leader of size has shared that out of necessity, she trained herself to be more tentative and soft-spoken in order not to be accused of overwhelming or overpowering others. She stated that being fat and powerful was equated with being a bully among her colleagues. In the opinion of some professionals of size, troubling attributes that are assigned to them are not solely based on personality but physicality as well, whether or not that distinction is recognized.

On a regular basis, obese professionals report not being able to advance themselves in their careers. Overweight medical doctors relate being passed over for internships, residencies, and executive hospital administration; overweight teachers have been asked during job interviews how long they are able to stand and if they are fit enough to chase after students; top sales executives see people they trained pass them up for promotion because clients complain that they are huge and sweaty; university administrators are unable to be promoted no matter how well they do on their jobs because rumor has it that students are repulsed by them. Many believe that this more pointed prejudice occurs mostly because, more than average people, "professionals should know better". An attorney who represented an obese professional who was denied an advanced position with his company was told that the company administrators were concerned that something was inherently wrong with a healthcare worker who could not effectively manage his own weight or health; they viewed him as potentially unstable and not fully trustworthy because of his size. That these worthy professionals are judged more on the size of their bodies than on the quality of their work is a deeply wounding travesty.

In closing, these perspectives on obesity cover some of the more denigrating and demoralizing aspects of bias that large people of all ages confront daily. Fortunately, they are not the *only* experiences for overweight individuals. There are pockets of caring and considerate normal-weight and obese people the world over who do not reject persons of considerable size. These welcoming human beings may shine a light for other fellow travelers journeying toward increased awareness and insight about the stigma imposed on individuals who are obese. It is this author's hope that this narrative will assist in reframing the reader's previous perceptions, and in advancing the kindness and sensitivity deserved by every person of size...and by every person.

DISCUSSION QUESTIONS

Please describe why or why not when answering the questions below.

1. Would you ever date a fat person?
2. Do you think more fat people are sloppy or dirty than not?
3. As a general rule, are fat people lazier than thin people?
4. Do you think fat people are less physically appealing?
5. Do you believe fat people, including children, are responsible for their weight?
6. Are you disgusted by seeing fat people at the beach in bathing suits?
7. Would you ever take a picture of a fat person in an embarrassing moment and pass it on to your friends or post it online?
8. Do you think attempted humor and unflattering terms about fat people are funny?
9. Are you annoyed if a fat person is seated near you and takes up more space?
10. Do you think outgoing and friendly fat people are obnoxious or gross?
11. Is there a difference between fat women and fat men?
12. Do you think fat people should exercise at a separate gym?
13. If you interviewed a fat person and a thin person with the exact same qualifications, which one would you hire?
14. Who would you offer to help carry a grocery bag for first: a thin elderly person or a fat elderly person?
15. Is a fat medical doctor as trustworthy as a thin doctor?

ACTIVITIES

- Revised Antifat Attitudes Scale http://www.jasonswrench.com/pdf/measures/antifat.pdf
- Fat Phobia Scale http://www.uconnruddcenter.org/resources/bias_toolkit/toolkit/Module-1/1-08-SelfAssessmentTools/1-0808-FatPhobia.pdf

SUGGESTED READINGS

- *Butter* by Erin Jade Lange
- *Fat Camp Commandos* by Daniel Pinkwater
- *Larger-Than-Life Lara* by Dandi Daley Mackall
- *Life in the Fat Lane* by Cherie Bennett
- *Looks* by Madeleine George

- *Losing It* by Erin Fry
- *The Middlesteins* by Jami Attenberg
- *One Fat Summer* by Robert Lipsyte
- *What's Wrong with Fat?* by Abigail C. Saguy

ANTIFAT PREJUDICE ASSOCIATIONS AND NETWORKS

- National Association to Advance Fat Acceptance (human rights)
- The Body Positive (transforming beliefs about weight and beauty)
- International Size Acceptance Association (education and advocacy)
- Council on Size & Weight Discrimination (nonprofit organization)
- Healthy Weight Network (news, commentary, links, and more)
- *NoLose* (formerly the National Organization for Lesbians of Size)
- http://www.cswd.org/ (nonprofit organization, Counsel on Size and Weight Discrimination)
- https://www.sizediversityandhealth.org/ (nonprofit organization, Assoc. of Size Diversity and Health)
- http://www.obesity.org/home (nonprofit, The Obesity Society)

OTHER WEB SITES ON ANTIFAT PREJUDICE

- Fat!So? (for people who don't apologize for their size)
- Obesity Law & Advocacy Center (representing obese people)
- Rudd Center for Food Policy and Obesity (Yale University)
- Making It Big (supporting the right of all women to be comfortable)

FILMS

- Bridget Jones's Diary (2001)
- Norbit (2007)
- Paul Blart: Mall Cop (2009)
- Shallow Hal (2001)
- Super Size Me (2004)
- What's Eating Gilbert Grape (1993)

NANCY LA MONICA

19. THE PEN STOPS[1]

"The pen stops? What do you mean the pen stops?" Jules interrupts the story just as I start telling it.

Taken by surprise, my mind wanders. My anxiety heightens as it often does when I share my experiences of being a person who is non-visibly disabled by and in academia. I catch myself looking over my shoulder to make sure no one is lurking. I'm careful not to name names even though we're meeting at least 60 kilometres away from a university. I'm not sure why I am worried about other people. Perhaps it has something to do with the feeling of being under surveillance, which I've felt since I disclosed my disability to a few administrators at a university a couple of months ago. One administrator said, "I hear everything".

And so, I feel watched, judged, oppressed in this place.

It is from this place that the story, my story, our story begins.

***

I start doodling in my notebook and I say, "Yes. The counselor just stopped writing".

I feel Jules staring at me with curiosity, waiting for me to continue. A sudden chill comes in from a draft that seeps from the front doors of Francie's Coffee Shop[2]. I need to pause. I ignore the stare by focusing my attention on the busy parking lot. I pick up my grande pumpkin spice latté, savouring each sip because doing so gives me a moment to collect myself. I need time to process my thoughts before I say more about my own – often very difficult – experiences in academia. I learned to cope in stressful situations by drinking gulps of water and coffee when I am speaking in public, to slow down my speech, so I apply this technique in many face-to-face encounters. I worry about how others perceive me, so I'm careful about what I say about these experiences, and how I say it. I don't want to be accused of sounding dramatic. This is especially true when I speak to people with whom I've shared my disability. Unless you've experienced what I have at the university, I'll worry about how you'll respond to my stories.

P. Leavy (Ed.), Privilege Through the Looking-Glass, 143–154.

***

To: lamonican@gmail.com
Re: Request for Research Participants

[…] I wish I had time to participate in your project because I think it's a very worthwhile and politically important project that may hopefully change attitudes around accessibility and dis/ability at [the university] and maybe other universities. As I'm sure you know from your other participants, it's hard being crip in school. This is exactly why I don't have time or energy to participate.[3]

I'm disheartened. But I can relate to this potential participant. This is why I started this project for my dissertation. There are far too many students out there experiencing the extra work of being disabled, and I'm one of them. My research explores the experiences of non-visibly disabled graduate students by examining how they negotiate both academic and workplace accommodations. I plan to illuminate the processes of disablement in academic spaces with the assertion that non-visibly disabled students' participation involves extra work. I argue that this extra work requires laborious efforts, both physically and psychologically for disabled students, and can be detrimental to their academic progress. For instance, disabled students must engage in time-consuming tasks associated with getting accommodated in the classroom and in their workplace. Such work can have physical costs when this exacerbates their impairments and disability by causing fatigue, for example. The physical manifestations of this extra work can also be emotional, threatening the student's self-esteem. Undertaking this kind of emotion work can affect a student's academic performance (Goode, 2007, p. 43) and might lead to academic burnout, even causing some students to drop out of their programs. I write back,

To: anonymous student
Re: Re: Request for Research Participants

No worries. Concentrate on your health and studies. Take good care and keep me posted. If there is anything I can do, please feel free to contact me.

***

"Hi Jules. It's Nancy. I just got your e-mail. I'm so sorry to read that you can't participate in the study, but I completely understand".

Jules isn't real – well, no, that's not really true. Jules is a composite character that I made up to represent various lived experiences and stories of the co-participants in my doctoral research who contributed to this broader conversation. Jules is the single voice that exclaims their experiences in a way that would not identify them (Chang, Wambura Ngunjiri, & Hernandez, 2013, p. 126). Jules is the vehicle that gives a voice where disability is often not paid attention.

Jules goes on, "Actually, I just couldn't handle academia anymore. My body took a beating. My health was compromised, and I tried to get medical leave. Twice in fact, but they gave me the runaround and I just couldn't do it anymore. It really messed up my head. My supervisory committee was supportive: they wrote letters on my behalf and checked in regularly with me. But there was nothing more they could do to help.

Long pause.

"My psychologist was surprised to learn of my decision to drop out. He knew how much I wanted to complete my doctorate. He wrote a few letters himself and gave a detailed summary about how this was affecting my overall health. I couldn't focus on my studies anymore. I also ended up lashing out at my family and friends over the smallest things. I didn't feel like myself. But after my last bout of depression and increased medication I didn't want to be on, I decided it was time to give up".

"What you're going through is the same story I've heard from other non-visibly disabled students regarding all the extra work they have to do to keep up. Sadly, it doesn't surprise me. I wish things were different and that there was an alternative solution, but I completely respect the decision you made. Self-care is so important. I'm not sure what to say other than, 'I'm sorry.' Is there anything I can do to help?"

"Actually, there is. That's why I e-mailed you. I thought about it, and I don't want to feel like all this work was for nothing. I know your study already started, but I'd really like to help with your research. I'd like to offer any support I can. Maybe I can be your sounding board? I know how isolating it can be to write a thesis. I wish I had turned to others for support".

"Wow, thanks! I think this is great and so wonderful of you to offer. I could use all the emotional and intellectual support I can get. I could definitely use a sounding board. I do hope that I can help get your voice heard. Your voice represents so many. It's vital to share your story".

From that day forward, we became comrades. We made Francie's Coffee Shop our second home, a place to meet and discuss my work. Part of Jules's supportive role has been to play devil's advocate and push me beyond my comfort zone in an effort to make my work better and, at the same time, provide emotional support on this journey.

***

Focus Nancy. Get back to how the pen stops. I'm having a hard time holding much of any focus today. My mind keeps wandering elsewhere. These stories are painful to retell. Over the years, I've had to learn to mentally train myself to focus back on the conversation, but this isn't easy. This is especially true when I become frustrated with retelling painful lived experiences.

Jules is aware of my focus issues; we share similar characteristics because we both have lived experiences with ADHD.[4] I'm told that this is all a part of my impairment, I recall telling Jules. Medically, I'm labeled as "severely" ADHD. My attention span is weak; I'm impulsive; my mind doesn't stop racing. I'm perceived as having a problem in my body and mind when, for example, I can't sit still. As if that wasn't enough to impact my academic performance at school, I also have a learning disability. *Of course, this is my problem, right? No, not really.* I'm awakened from what feels like a trance, typical of my overactive brain, by Jules's snapping fingers.

"Hey, where'd you go? What'd you mean the pen stopped at the counselor's office? I'm still confused about the whole notion of disability accommodations at the graduate level as it is. I never visited the counseling office for accommodations. I was too ashamed. I mean, seriously, they have the same counselors that my own students use. I didn't want to be seen at the counseling office especially when I wasn't even sure if I was eligible for accommodations. What if one of my students saw me? I just couldn't do it. I tried. Several times, actually. Each time, I made it a bit further: first, I reached the second floor; next, the third; and finally, I made it to the front door, but then I quickly turned back. That was it. I figured if I made it this far to reach grad school, I should be able to complete my studies without accommodations. If I couldn't get through grad school without them, I really shouldn't be there in the first place. Right?"

"I can relate to how you're feeling, Jules, but I respectfully have to disagree. Why shouldn't disabled grads get accommodations? Research shows that accommodations are essential for students, including disabled graduate students. Yes, they can do the work. They have the "intellectual smarts," however you care to define that. Why shouldn't they be able to access grad school? If it takes a person twice as long to mark essays because of their processing speeds, they're actually working twice the hours as another student for the same pay! There are lots of ways we could make accommodations happen. I tried to explain this to the counselor the first time I met at their office to register as a student with a disability and access my accommodations. Well, what I mean is when I *tried* to register".

"Tried to register? What do you mean? What happened?"

"It's funny, you know," I say, mentally placing myself back in the registrar's office, "I imagined this highly bureaucratic process would be relatively smooth because I'm familiar with it. Not to mention, I'm both a student and researcher of this process, too. I mean, I have a ton of knowledge about accommodations in academia. I've been exploring disability issues throughout my university career: serving on accessibility committees, taking courses in disability studies – I did my master's degree in disability studies – mentoring other students, being a disability ally and advocate. Oh, yeah, and I am also disabled.

"Still, I found myself apprehensive about meeting with the counselor as a graduate student. During our consultation, I asked the counselor about workplace accommodations for disabled graduates like myself. The counselor seemed unsure of any accommodations provided for disabled grads and suggested that medical programs offer modified work placements for disabled students, but that was about as much as I could get in terms accessing information. It was like pulling teeth".

This experience brought back the feelings of complete frustration when I first acquired the knowledge of my disability and first requested accommodations from the university. "The counselor asked me what accommodations I'd need. How should I know? I was just identified as a disabled. 'Don't you have a checklist of the accommodations you offer?' I asked defensively. I was given a speech about how accommodations are individualized, that there was no such thing as a checklist of accommodation options, and that if the university provided one, all disabled students would take advantage of accommodations that they might not otherwise need".

"Take advantage?! Is that how they saw us, as taking advantage?!" Jules exclaims.

I couldn't help but remember how angry and powerless I felt as an undergraduate student with little to no knowledge of my rights to accessible higher education. Only this time was different. I knew my rights as a graduate student – sort of, anyway – and I was prepared to fight for them. You bet your ass I did my research beforehand.

"Yeah, it's frustrating that they treat us that way, especially when the research shows that disabled grads need institutions to offer things like reduced teaching loads, the recognition of doctoral research as fulfilling the research workload, fewer or no committee responsibilities, especially at critical times in doctoral work (Dunn, Haines, Hardie, Leslie, & MacDonald, 2008, "Employment Equity and Supports," para. 4).

"And I did exactly what they ask of students in the policy: I consulted my counselor about any concerns about meeting the 'essential requirements' of the academic program. I went to the disability services department before I registered. I talked to profs about any concerns they may have about my ability to meet the program requirements. And still, with all this under my belt, the counselor wasn't able to address my concerns, let alone tell me whom I could speak to about these concerns – concerns that would impact my academic progress in the program".

A quick Google search reveals that these are the typical guidelines for students to access accommodations. I had made sure to read and follow the policies pertaining to academic accommodations. So why, then, was I having a difficult time navigating information for disabled graduates in their role as academic workers? Turns out that, for the most part, the accommodation policy is predominately for academic work such as extensions for submitting assignments. What about workplace accommodations? I couldn't find information about who disabled graduate students consult if this is, in fact, a different process from the student academic accommodation process. If information about access to accommodations wasn't "easily" available to me when I accepted entrance to my academic program, how was I to know how to navigate this process?

Like many graduate students, I was offered a stipend and scholarship through the university that required me to work as a teaching assistant.[5] While this is typical for "many" graduate students, it might differ from one department to the next. By accepting this offer, I'd be considered an employee of the university, protected by a collective agreement. Consequently, I had anticipated the counselor's role would include helping me understand the processes for both academic and workplace accommodations. This wasn't actually the case because the counselor knew very little about workplace accommodations. Surely, I couldn't be the only disabled graduate student who needed this kind of information. If my counselor had no knowledge of workplace accommodations, how was I to find out if not by this office? Who then would be my disability advocate?[6] Did such an advocate even exist? I found myself becoming more and more frustrated about this subject with the counselor.

***

Early in the intake process, the counselor literally stopped writing. I became aware of my own anxiety. I shifted in my seat, the heat of my breath quickening my statements, matching my quickening pulse. The chatter that occupies my mind daily is what got me into trouble that day: just before the counselor's pen stopped, I blurted out, in an offhand way, that I had met with a new psychologist last month: "His report will be ready for me to pick up in a few weeks, so I'll get this to your office soon," I told the counselor.

That was it.

The pen just stopped.

Abruptly closing the manila folder where notes were handwritten, the counselor stared blankly at me and stopped writing altogether with no explanation. I stared back wondering what just happened. *Did I say something wrong?* I felt my heart sink. The room was spinning. I temporarily blanked out for a few seconds while I watched the counselor's lips move. The counselor explained that the university requires the most recent psychological medical documentation before any student can be registered as a student with a disability.[7]

Wait. What? I'm puzzled. Clearly, this is just a misunderstanding. I provided all the necessary medical documentation in addition to a pile of accommodation letters from my previous institution when only one was required. I might have provided too much. I had studied the university's policy before I made the appointment so that I knew I'd be prepared.

What's wrong with the medical documentation I've already provided? That documentation is within the five-year validation period. I remember that my chest felt hot and I was sure it was visibly beaming red from my modest v-neck t-shirt.

That documentation is a part of my embodied disability – a constant reminder of being labeled – a constant reminder of the emotional and physical fatigue I experienced after fighting with the university for six months straight, knocking on university administrators' doors to help me get a provincial bursary to pay for the $1850 psycho-educational assessment.[8] Do you know how many disabled students cannot access their accommodations because they cannot financially afford, much less emotionally afford, this assessment that the university requires?

For an assessment, that, I should add, demoralized me by making me answer questions about American history at the age of 27; a subject about which I had no recollection. I recall throwing unanswered math equations back to the assessor because I can't do math without a calculator. I completed timed writing and reading exercises, and played with building blocks, feeling like a seven-year-old, over the course of 20 hours.

The assessment allows medical professionals like this psychologist to pathologize me, reproducing the notion of normalcy (Davis, 1995). He chose his words very carefully when he advised me to not pursue a career in teaching because of my "lack of organizational skills" and apparent "severe ADHD". Adding to the insult, his assistant probed me as to why I wanted to continue my grad studies, asking whether I was trying to prove something to someone or myself, offering advice I never solicited, telling me I have nothing to prove and should choose another career path.

Another career path.

I remember wanting to leave that office right away, feeling shame, fear, and regret. Why did I put myself through this crap anyway? Maybe they're right, I thought to myself. Maybe teaching wasn't something I should or even could do.

***

"You're telling me the assessment I handed you when I came in is not enough to register me today as a disabled student?" I asked the counselor.

The counselor appeared empathetic to my situation, even apologetic, reiterating that there was nothing that could be done to proceed until the office received my most recent documentation.

I am angry with myself because I couldn't stop myself from talking impulsively; I shouldn't have mentioned the recent report in the first place. If I hadn't opened my chatty mouth about this new doctor, the counselor wouldn't have known and I'd be registered as a "student with a disability" and on my way home instead of feeling completely anxious.

I'm outraged.

Deep breathe in; slow breath out.

Silence.

I work hard to slow my breath down. I can't show my anger; I don't want to be perceived as someone with emotional or anger issues. I clear my voice, gather my papers back into my manila folder and tell the counselor it was nice to meet them.

I quietly leave the office and immediately call my friend to vent my disbelief about what just happened.

***

Jules is soaking up this story like a sponge. Retelling my story recalls emotions of frustration, failure, anger, and pain. I'm sure it conjures memories for Jules as well. I was right.

"I'd like to say 'That's unbelievable,' but I am not that surprised by any of this. When I first read about your study, I was taken aback because I didn't think there were that many people in grad studies with disabilities. At least not, you know, disabilities that aren't obvious. Disabilities like yours and mine. I mean, I know there are things in place for wheelchair users, like accessible washrooms, if you're really lucky! I've heard it's possible to ask for accessible classrooms. But accommodations for LDs and mental health? Really?"

"Well, actually," I pause. "The number of students like us, and students with other kinds of disabilities, is on the rise. I read an OECD report published in 2003 that said anti-discrimination legislation is part of the reason for disabled persons pursuing degrees in post-secondary education. I assume that part of the reason there are more disabled students is that accommodations are understood to be a human right now. But we have such a long way to go before we break through the barriers that still exist and prevent full inclusionary spaces (Damiani & Harbour, 2015; Olkin, 2002). This is especially true for disabled grad students. As we both know, there's just not enough research out there".

"Yeah, you can say that again!"

"And that's because research tends to focus on undergrads (OMET, 1998; Rose, 2009). And even then, their voices continue to be absent from the literature. That's not to say undergrads aren't important. I'm just saying we need to get a better picture of how disabled grads experience academia as inclusionary and/or as exclusionary (Farrar, 2004; Rose, 2009). This is important for so many reasons!"

"Yeah, and without the proper supports in place, well, we've both heard about colleagues who couldn't progress in their studies and chose to drop out as a result of poor accommodations".

"I reference Marilyn Rose's work a lot. It's called *Accommodating Graduate Students with Disabilities,* and she presented to the Council of Ontario Universities. She talks about the high cost of failing to accommodate disabled students, like 'the loss of talent to society' when disabled students don't graduate. And then, my personal favourite, she talks about 'the loss of self-esteem and potential income for disabled students who can't keep up' – whatever that means." (Parks, Antonoff, Drake, Skiba, & Soberman as cited in Rose, 2009, pp. 5–6).

"Not to mention that grad students are often also employees of the university while they are working toward their doctorates. If they can't manage the full load of teaching and research assistantships, they might lose out on the scholarship money that is attached to those positions with the university".

"Yeah. I know. That's exactly what motivated this project in the first place, Jules. I have been so involved in listening to students' stories about access to accommodations. I'm so passionate about this topic because it's not just personal; it's also political. I don't want to point fingers, but I do want to learn from these experiences even if they are hard to hear. No one wants to think that they've been a part of someone's oppressive experience, of course. But if we don't get the students' voices out and heard, how will anything change for the better? And, seriously, I want to hear about the positive experiences too.

"We already know that LDs and mental health disabilities are among the most prevalent disabilities documented among university students (OECD, 2003), but they are still very much stigmatized and misunderstood. I hear from many disabled students that they think they're 'taking advantage of the system,' (Denhart, 2008; Hibbs & Pothier, 2006) as if accommodations are some sort of special treatment. Of course, we know that accommodations are not special treatment; it's an entitlement to barrier-free learning. I mean, the bottom line is, access to higher learning shouldn't be laborious work, as it currently can be. Why do disabled students need to do work to get accommodated? Sorry, that was a mouthful".

"No worries. I get it. Passion is what is going to get you through your doctorate."

My pen stops. I smile.

DISCUSSION QUESTIONS

1. How is access to education a privilege?
2. Where is oppression hidden in academia?
3. What is the difference between an accommodation and privilege?
4. Imagine one of your peers disclosed a disability to you. Would you perceive your peer as having an advantage over your learning opportunities?
5. What barriers exist for students who need accommodations in your college/university?

6. What do inclusionary spaces look like in your learning spaces?

SUGGESTED READING

Morella-Pozzi, D. (2014). The (dis)ability double life: Exploring legitimacy, illegitimacy, and the terrible dichotomy of (dis)ability in higher education. In R. M. Boylorn & M. P. Orbe (Eds.), *Critical autoethnography: Intersecting cultural identities in everyday life* (pp. 176–188). Left Coast Press, Inc.

Titchkosky, T. (2011). *The question of access: Disability, space, meaning.* University of Toronto Press.

NOTES

[1] This reflects Chapter One: The Pen Stops of my thesis entitled "Surviving or thriving in academia: Autoethnographic accounts of non-visibly disabled grads' experiences of inclusion and exclusion" and is supported by the Social Sciences and Humanities Research Council, 2012-2014 [752-2012-2030].

[2] Francie's Coffee Shop is a fictional name.

[3] Any e-mails shared have been done so with permission.

[4] ADHD is often medicalized, "[as] a disorder of the central nervous system (CNS) characterized by disturbances in the areas of attention, impulsiveness, and hyperactivity" (Kelly & Ramundo, 2006, p. 14). Disability scholars and others, however, reject this medical label, noting that the so-called symptoms of ADHD can be sources of creativity and energy. See for example, La Monica & Chouinard, 2013. See also Goodley, 2011, p. 147.

[5] To the best of my knowledge, it is typical for graduate students in Canada to be offered stipends or scholarships in their academic programs. However, the amount of funding can differ significantly in how much a student might be funded (e.g., from a few thousand dollars to tens of thousands of dollars).

[6] A disability advocate can be described as someone who supports disabled students in navigating accommodation barriers to access in their college/university.

[7] Since the time of this writing, there has been a significant change to the accommodation process for disabled students in Ontario. Please see: http://www.ohrc.on.ca/en/news_centre/new-documentation-guidelines-accommodating-students-mental-health-disabilities.

[8] The cost of a full psycho-educational assessment varies depending on province. At some universities, assessments are completed internally, but students could find themselves on a minimum of a six-month waiting list for an initial appointment. Depending on their available funding opportunities, some students endure the financial costs to take this (required) medical testing in order to establish a need for accommodations (Hibbs & Pothier, 2003, p. 203). Students must provide proof of disability to obtain any type of formal disability-related accommodation request. This requires a student to accept and disclose their impairment and/or disability to a university because "self-identifying as disabled, sets the disability policy in motion" (Jung, 2003, p. 102). In 2007, at the time of my assessment, the cost for such an assessment was $1,850 in Ontario, Canada.

REFERENCES

Damiani, M., & Harbour, W. (2015). Being the wizard behind the curtain: Teaching experiences of graduate teaching assistants with disabilities at U.S. universities. *Innovative Higher Education, 40*(5), 399–413. doi:10.1007/s10755-015-9326-7

Davis, L. J. (1995). *Enforcing normalcy: Disability, deafness, and the body.* New York, NY & London: Verso.

Denhart, H. (2008). Deconstructing barriers: Perceptions of students labeled with learning disabilities in higher education. *Journal of Learning Disabilities, 41*(6), 483–497.

Dunn, P., Hanes, R., Hardie, S., Leslie, D., & MacDonald, J. (2008). Best practices in promoting disability inclusion within Canadian schools of social work. *Disability Studies Quarterly, 28*(1), 1–10.

Farrar, V. (2004). *Access to research: Institutional issues for disabled postgraduate research students.* Newcastle upon Tyne: University of Newcastle. Retrieved from http://www.vitae.ac.uk/CMS/files/upload/Premia-Access-to-research-institutional-issues-for-disabled-research-students-March-2004.pdf

Goode, J. (2007). 'Managing' disability: Early experiences of university students with disabilities. *Disability & Society, 22*(1), 35–48.

Goodley, D. (2011). *Disability studies: An interdisciplinary introduction.* London: Sage Publications, Inc.

Hibbs, T., & Pothier, D. (2006). Post-Secondary education and disabled students: Mining a level playing field or playing in a minefield? In D. Pothier & R. Devlin (Eds.), *Critical Disability theory: Essays in philosophy, politics, policy and law* (pp. 195–219). British Columbia: The University of British Columbia Press.

Jung, K. E. (2003). Chronic illness and academic accommodation: Meeting disabled students' "unique needs" and preserving the institutional order of the university. *Journal of Sociology & Social Welfare, 30*(1), 91–112.

Kelly, K., & Ramundo, P. (2006). *You mean I'm not lazy, stupid or crazy?* New York, NY: Scribner.

La Monica, N., & Chouinard, V. (2013). Warning: Labels may cause serious side effects for learning disabled students. In A. Azzopardi (Ed.), *Youth: Responding to lives – an international handbook* (pp. 193–209). Sense Publishers.

Olkin, R. (2002). The rights of graduate psychology students with disabilities. *Journal of Social Work in Disability & Rehabilitation, 1*(1), 67–80.

Ontario Human Rights Commission. (2016, January 06). *New documentation guidelines for accommodating students with mental health disabilities.* Retrieved from http://www.ohrc.on.ca/en/news_centre/new-documentation-guidelines-accommodating-students-mental-health-disabilities

Ontario Ministry of Education and Training. (1998, October). *Removing the barriers to graduate and professional education and careers: Report from the AGAPE committee (Access to Graduate and Professional Education).*

Organisation for Economic Co-Operation and Development. (2003). *Disability in higher education.* Paris: OECD Publications Service.

Rose, M. (November 2009). *Accommodating graduate students with disabilities* (Council of Ontario Universities Academic Colleagues Working Paper) (pp. 1–21). Ontario: Brock University.

MIROSLAV PAVLE MANOVSKI

20. RESPONSIVE STORIES

Sharing Evocative Tales from the Inside, Out

It is important to find ways to make time for reflective processes in our ever-busy lives. We all live within a culture and our socio-cultural ways of being are laden with beliefs and norms that may or may not be optimal for autonomous, safe, or free apprenticeship learning experiences with young people or their stakeholders. Let us take time to imagine just one young child in school: it would benefit us to take into account their favorite way to engage or participate in learning, mindful of the world in which they lived before our collaborative interaction. Such a world may or may not include experience with their family or home environment, including guardians, parents, siblings, and extended families. Their prior experience may or may not include events in their neighborhood, from shopping centers, playgrounds, or interactions with peers, neighbors, and social/cultural groups we expect them to have had.

We could also imagine that this neighborhood is next to another, part of a larger community (e.g., law enforcement, medical doctors, lawyers, religious institutions), and it would behoove us to find connections to how we live and play amid and with collaborators of our world. Further, it may not improve our experience to assume all learners have had the same or similarly shared experience, or to accept that generalizations, social stereotypes, current/prior stigmas, or status associations that distinguish *them* versus *us* let us work toward the *we* in learning and honor the multifariousness that each person brings to the collaborative learning forum.

An approach toward such processes of inquiry may be to begin with our own stories and ways of expressions (manovski, 2013, 2014), creating approaches to solve puzzles concerning negative realities in school and beyond that are normalized – routinely built upon from prior hardships endured and neglected, assigned, budding, or inherited – that ignore the holistic process of the social-cultural ecology of our development. Too often we witness and abide harmful realities arising between family, community, neighborhood,

P. Leavy (Ed.), Privilege Through the Looking-Glass, 155–164.

school, and global circles, bottling up tensions until an emergency pushes to rebellion or other extremes. What other options may we invest or time and efforts in? How may we implement them and why?

***

I was congratulated for being chosen to be part of a diversity committee for one of the public schools and districts for which I have previously worked. It wasn't a group I volunteered to be part of, rather, one I was appointed to (despite other willing people wanting to be part of the group). Chosen people from the whole district met in a large conference room and were encouraged to be willing participants in ways that deepened our understanding of culturally responsive teaching (Gay, 2010). We collaborated and innovated for five or six full-day sessions throughout the school year. In that time, we created a personal taxonomy of words about social justice; fleshed out our in-the-moment awareness of cultural competency via think and write/ pair and share community builders; worked with Four "A"s Text Protocols that exemplified our assumptions, our arguments, our agreements, and our aspirations; took notes on provided scholarly/non-scholarly articles and YouTube videos; utilized personal journaling; documented what we saw, what we thought, and what we wondered from emergent feelings during our sessions that focused on racial/ethnic social identities, and more. We also were asked to switch seats and groups, worked against a stopwatch, and were often challenged to work away from people we knew or wanted to spend more time with. Though many people were happy to be part of this committee, much of their fondness seemed to recede in time. As I wondered how our professional lives in schools aligned with our personal loves outside of schools, our facilitators would remind us that what we got out of our experience together was dependent upon what we put into our experience together. We were expected to facilitate versions of these events with the staff at our respective schools.

During one of our sessions, many people were told that they had spent a good deal of time deepening their knowledge of practice and developing their knowledge about students, parents, and guardians, yet they did not necessarily have a deeper understanding of themselves. This included what they intentionally or unintentionally brought to their learning world from their own prior experience. We were asked to consider why knowing more about our own prior experience may be of importance. Someone shared that they were afraid to stray from our overtly detailed curricula – that dealing with all the baggage we carry made them feel uncomfortable and nervous – mindful of evaluation expectations from those in power, and always afraid of losing their job. They continued by sharing they would rather be told what to do and how to do it, in order to avoid reprimand. Our facilitator wondered aloud if bridging that gap of concern may or may not be part of affecting the achievement of our students in our classrooms (Gardner, 2006), and I contemplated the journey ahead: what themes would emerge and would the whispers from others at my table represent the thoughts and perceptions of the rest of the people in the room? More complex, once we learned what they had to teach us, how would the staff at our school embrace what we had to teach them? How would it be implemented? How would it be accounted for? Who would benefit from such efforts, and what ramifications would arise if our execution or outcomes were unfavorable?

Aside from my concerns, a pleasing moment surfaced when we focused on learning more about social identity groups. Though there are numerous resources that generally explain that these groups are based on physical, social, and mental characteristics of individuals, I didn't know much about this topic until I was asked to document my own identities (using a worksheet of a blank Social Identity Wheel adapted from "Voices Discovery," Intergroup Relations Center, Arizona State University). I became fascinated and felt thrown off balance from all my emerging feelings. For example, we were all asked to document our gender, sex, race, ethnicity, sexual orientation/attraction, religion/spirituality or faith/meaning, social class, age, [dis]ability, nation of origin and/or citizenship, tribal or indigenous affiliation, and body size/type. Then, we were asked to consider which identities we thought about most often, least often, which identities we'd like to learn more about, and which identities have the strongest effect on how you see yourself as a person and why. Finally, we were asked which identities were permanent and which we could throw away or ignore.

Soon, I was noticing that some social identity groups were obvious and clear, and some were not obvious and were unclear, and often self-claimed or frequently ascribed by others. I learned that the majority of the people, who shared more of the common, majority, or "normal" identities, became part of an *agent group* or social identity group that held unearned privileges, and that the other *target groups* or social identity groups were potentially disenfranchised and exploited. As I was about to burst from glee from finally making this connection from something that seemed so obvious, yet new to me, it was time to enjoy our provided lunch. Though it was our fifth or so session and we had been asked if we had any special dietary needs, I was informed that they did not provide a vegan option for me (because I was the only one and it was too much trouble for them). I had to leave the group, buy my own lunch, and return within our short, allotted break. I ended up late as there was no parking available when I returned, and the rest of my session somehow wasn't as meaningful.

***

She often has meltdowns. They seem to increase in frequency and severity. Within seconds of her smiling, she hits herself in the head, bangs her feet against walls or kicks whatever or whomever is near. Even though I have not received an IEP or 504 for this person (many professionals had trouble coming to an agreement about classifying or labeling her, and services would not be provided until a consensus was reached), she is one of a handful of students who doesn't seem to be receiving the care they need. She also didn't seem to be learning anything in school, and I wondered if this was the best place for her. I certainly was not told her confidential history or story; that information was only for the general classroom teacher. I have not been informed of whether or not a paraprofessional should be with her at all times or not, but when meltdowns occurred, nobody follows up or does anything to document what happened. Instead, I am simply to escort my entire class out of the room and wait for someone else to arrive. We usually hang out in the hallway or in the multipurpose room. Sometimes there is a class in there, so we join other students in the library and wait for an all-clear. During one of these waiting times, a classroom teacher whispered to me, "She stays because we receive loads more money for special needs students than regular students". I feel a bit spacey and dry-mouthed, not quite sure what to say. I just nod.

When I return, my room is usually a mess and sometimes instruments are broken. Xylophones have been thrown and turned over. Students' folders are thrown all over the room. Tables and chairs are knocked over and recorders are strewn throughout. A couple of drum skins are punched through and some maracas are crushed. Though I am told that all damaged instruments will be replaced, I know that they will not be and that I am being pacified. I try to imagine what causes such destruction and what such a person must be going through, and I wonder what more we may do to healthfully help her. I also see that she often has bite marks all over her arms and sometimes on her legs, and I wonder if she will bite others; I wonder what I am to do if she bites me or another student in my class. I observe that she is also covered in large bruises. She smells like urine and appears unwashed. She wears the same clothes to school with different colored ribbons in her hair. I hope that music and the arts may somehow be a gateway to enabling positive opportunities for this person, connections between both our worlds and knowings. I try to create connections with her within the short time we have together, while maintaining my efforts to meaningfully conduct lessons and learning for everyone in my class. I'm not sure if anything I am doing is helping and I feel exhausted.

In time, the other students are no longer afraid when she starts to get physically aggressive or mutters terrible threats and swear words. She continues to get mad at herself and is no longer able to go out for recess, because she just keeps running and they're afraid that she'll leave the school grounds. She starts to breathe heavily and loudly when she is angry or upset. She becomes less aware of other peoples' personal space and starts to have electrified spasms in her body when she is unable to express what she is thinking or when she is asked to partake in lessons. She starts to spit. She starts to growl. She turns over tables and throws metal chairs across the room. She ignores all directions toward safety and calm and she refuses to take a break. We are not allowed to touch her. She starts to take off her clothes and wildly licks her mouth in circles. She giggles and screams.

No one is answering my phone calls to the office, to her homeroom teacher's line, or to the Special Needs room, so we all exit the room. It's February and we still do not have a healthful plan in place for this person and other people like her. I wonder if any plan would work? She is naked and screaming at the top of her lungs as the last few students gawk and reluctantly leave the music room; they want to see what else she'll do. I realize that it's almost time for after school Honor's Choir rehearsal, and I wonder where we will rehearse and if we will be able to get the piano there in time. I instantly feel guilty to have such thoughts and feel like a selfish person. I notice some poor behaviors from some of my students in the hallway, so I ask two or three of them to stop mimicking her; they seem unable to control their giggling and laughing, and I realize I'm having trouble breathing.

I do not know why she is screaming and naked, though I do feel that I too could start screaming from the terrible situations that have been allowed to fester concerning the educational affairs in Michigan and beyond. From legislators who have no expertise in education yet claim to support education, to overemphasized standards and grading procedures that negatively impact the process and experience of learning that should be fun and inspirational, to the rampant bullying intersecting administration, teachers, parents, students, and those people in-between, to the pay cuts that no longer afford me the opportunity to live near the districts I have had the privilege to work in...

dark days seem to be settling in. I wonder how many more days until summer break, as if some healing may then begin. I have nightmares. I wonder if I should remain in this profession. I feel like a lonely and losing warrior, and I realize I've begun to binge eat every evening after school. I think of the array of personalities and experiences I navigate, and commiserate with other colleagues that *get it*. They tell me that she and others like her are staying at our school, that more like her are coming, and that they may be removed from art, dance, foreign language, music, physical education, and recess, and that a padded room has been created to keep them and others safe. Morning, noon, and night, I think about my job. I think, *Of course these students should be in our school, but how can I improve the experience for all?* I wonder if life really does get better for some and I wonder if I am making a positive difference or not in these wonderful students' lives. I then think about my own practice outside of school and leaf through the music I am working on for an upcoming performance. I have trouble shaking off the events from earlier in my day.

***

Reflecting, I imagine that abuse and oppression may unfold for each of us in a variety of ways. I observe and ponder how these events affect our experience and development in myriad learning moments. Even for those that feel their lives are free from harm, I wonder how we may approach healthful ways of breaching singular beliefs and truths that may narrow perspectives, impede apprenticeships, and upset the balance between degrees of logic and reason from emotion and feeling. Considering the large and shifting field of stewards guiding people through an array of disciplines within education, scaffolding learners and stakeholders within the complexities shaping our shared happenings, I inquire how a phenomenon that reinforces insensitivity to global ways of being may further diminish our ability to ponder, review, and question those creating, interpreting, and placing value on research intersecting daily life of people in schools and beyond.

For example, how may we encourage people to take time to analyze their growing web of life experience, and why should we engage in such processes? Could we honor and make salubrious room for multiple ways of expression – imagining how people may re-share their authentic prior experience between objective and subjective approaches – and how should we critique those portrayal meanings that tale perspectives of life intricacies? Could emergent deliberation from such events be of use and how could those be grappled with in ways that positively enrich humanity? How and why should we consider investing our time and efforts to become more compassionate, caring, empathic, and patient, aiming to become increasingly aware of people/voices negatively marginalized in schools, and why would identifying contributing patterns of harm enhance all our lives? From all we make sense of, what shall we do, why shall we do it, and how shall we work to stop detrimental behaviors and musings?

Taking time to investigate difficult or taboo episodes may positively enable us to construct an understanding of those complexities that negatively contribute to detrimental processes or outcomes. Moreover, the prospect of studying routine hurts from prior experience may be worthwhile and perhaps deeply meaningful if unfolded or retold in *artful ways*. Those evolving methods may also coax unexpected collaborations as people encourage one another to seek out experts or people who resonate alongside current knowings, slogging in the direction of more desirable conditions. However, some people enduring hardships may exist without champions, sidling isolation and loneliness, and it may seem impossible to conceptualize options of rescue from embedded wreckage. Still, let us probe for ways that may propel healthful alternatives that may not have been realized or embraced, making connections with others in ways that may make tangible far away dreams or beneficial affinities.

Though embarking on quests that provide circumstances to bridge gaps in our thinking is often accompanied by uncertainty and tension, let us acknowledge the degree of joy and privilege we embody – away from maintaining misconceptions and perspectives that misguide, or in-the-box processes that fashion participatory moments away from multiple truths and ambivalence – by encouraging schemes that spur empowerment of deserving lives, opportunities curated toward illuminating social-cultural justice occurrences. I urge you to share your story and to willingly heed the stories that are a part of your world.

ACTIVITIES

1. Generate a list of norms or behaviors that you think would be needed to make a safe and inclusive learning/living environment for you. Next, write a memorable story from your prior experience, working to remain authentic and genuine as it unfolded in real time. Be sure to include details about this time in history and include other affinities: your favorite routines,

movies, events, music, seasons, or holidays... or relevant hardships. Be sure to disclose what you remember with certainty and how you are so certain, and what parts of the story you may need to confirm and how you could do that. Then, review your story and check to see if any of the norms on your list were embedded in your story. Make note of what you feel and notice. When you and a partner are ready, share your story and list of norms with each other, documenting what each of you noticed from what you shared. Were your norms the same? Were your stories similar? Were either list of norms embedded in either of your stories? Did more insights emerge later and what were they? During and after your collaboration, document any alterations you wish would have emerged or been part of your prior experience and *why* you have included those alterations today. Finally, journal how you felt while embarking on this process, adding any thoughts you may have to make the exercise more meaningful and useful, closing with thoughts showcasing what you have learned and what may or may not have been positively influenced by your past or potential future experience from this activity.

a. As an extension, consider creating artful works that represent your story, and when possible, showcase your processes and any other collaboration that may emerge. If you are a person that works with music playing or if you doodle while you work, include those details and consider how such art may have been an underlying scaffold a part of this process: Do you think this may be significant?

2. With your colleagues/peers, define what stereotypes are. Then individually, make a list of stereotypes that you imagine exist or you have heard about from the following examples: African Americans, Asians, LGBTQ, Hispanic/Latinos, Jewish, Middle Eastern, special needs learners, or other labels that are meaningful to you.

Next, as a whole group, document what each member of the class has come up with. What are you able to notice? How do you think your stereotypes came to be and what other implications do you imagine? Are any of the stereotypes positive and if not, how may they be countered? Finally, define student/teacher bias and micro/macro aggressions. What other relevant connections are you able to make? How and why is it important to consider knowing more about this as a stakeholder of learning environments?

3. Visit an educational setting with your colleagues/peers after obtaining permission to embark on such a project (make sure all members who are a part of this experience agree to collaborating and being observed by you and your colleagues/peers). Make note of all the people in attendance.

Who do you notice and how do you describe them? What is the lesson that is being taught and why do you think the lesson is being taught? How are people learning in this setting and what problems arise, if any, during the learning process? What did you like? What would you do differently if you were the leader? How would you feel if you were the leader or the learner? What else are you thinking about as you are observing? Are you triggered to recall any of your prior experience during this process? Does anything unexpected take place and how are those unexpected events handled? Finally, debrief with your colleagues/peers and make note of everything that was observed by the group (consider recording these sessions in multiple ways, too). Next, after another day or two, work to retell the event without specifically identifying any person in ways that protects all participants from being pointed out. Why is this important? Is the story any less or more powerful? Does the story remain intact or does it stray from the original experience (review your materials and consider transcribing recordings)? Was anyone deleted or missed in the retelling? Why may that be or not be important from this work? What other questions or suggestions emerged from this experience? What lessons are of significance to you and potentially other audiences?

a. As an extension: what other processes in art were in play and perhaps taken for granted or what artful processes may enable a more evocative retelling of this experience, free from altering it in ways that may completely change the original emergent themes from the story? Could drawings be created? Could the story be fictionalized? Could music be composed? Could a short play be created, or a movie with players, or other artwork? Could a dance be choreographed? Could your audio or video notes be used in these artful ways? Why would such attempts be meaningful for people outside of this experience? What would need to be put in place in order to ethically proceed in ways that protect all stakeholders a part of such a project during the retelling? How shall its evolution maintain the essence of the experience and what teachable moments do you hope to healthfully enable? How may you anticipate unforeseen problems from this work and who may help you navigate the complexities ahead?

REFERENCES

Gardner, H. (2006). *Multiple intelligences: New horizons.* New York, NY: Basic Books.
Gay, G. (2010). *Culturally responsive teaching: Theory, research, and practice* (2nd ed.). New York, NY: Teachers College Press.

manovski, m. p. (2013). Snap-shot reflections: Targeting young boys singing girls' songs in schools. *GEMS (Gender, Education, Music and Society),* 6(3) 23–33.

manovski, m. p. (2014). *Arts-based research, autoethnography, and music education: Singing through a culture of marginalization.* Rotterdam, The Netherlands: Sense Publishers.

21. DEATH BY A THOUSAND CUTS

From Self-Hatred to Acceptance

Contrary to the superficial evidence, there is nothing simple about the structure and dynamics of racism...Its capacity to punctuate the universe into two great opposites masks something else; it masks the complexes of feelings and attitudes, beliefs and conceptions, that are always refusing to be so neatly stabilized and fixed...all that symbolic and narrative energy and work is directed to secure us 'over here' and them 'over there,' to fix each in its appointed species place.

(Stuart Hall qtd in Boyer 2011)

INTRODUCTION

I have never been enough: not thin enough, not pretty enough, not polite enough, not friendly enough, and certainly not white or black enough. Life has been a lesson in learning not to care, or at least dismissing "normality" as conformity. I chose non-conformity in every way I could, while trying to be "normal" and failing over and over and over. This is the story of my journey to a place where I can accept and face the world as it is, flawed and unfair, not how it should be, and finally accepting that I am fine just the way I am.

It's a strange thing to live in a world where people believe they know everything about you simply by looking, but that is the world as it is. Not all my problems stem from the color of my skin, but as my story reveals, it certainly formed the basis of my self-hatred, skewing my perception of the world around me, and hiding the roses of my past behind impenetrable thorns. Thus, my race was the core element of 'me' that I had to accept before I could ever begin the road to happiness. This chapter attempts to chart that journey by exploring the experiences I had in my formative years and in my work environments. While my experiences were very personal, my interactions with the world were/are indicative of the broader experiences of the marginalized.

P. Leavy (Ed.), Privilege Through the Looking-Glass, 165–182.
© *2017 Sense Publishers. All rights reserved.*

IN THE BEGINNING – "I HATE MYSELF AND WANT TO DIE"
(KURT COBAIN, 1993)

The first time I taught First Year Studies, I asked the students to interview their most important caregiver to find out how they really saw them. To model it, I interviewed my mother and brother.

I do not belong here.

Who should know and accept you better than your family? From their answers, it became clear that they didn't know me at all, proving my lifelong paranoid belief that I was incomprehensible and did not fit anywhere, not even in my own family. Of course, as they point out, the version of me that they knew was the version I gave them, so who is to blame that they didn't see me when I hid behind a constant, silent veil? They argue that I exaggerate the bad thus obscuring the good, and they are probably right. I hated myself so completely that it made perfect sense to believe that everyone else felt the same way about me, especially when neither action nor words belied my perceptions.

Thus, from the time I was four, I understood, or at least suspected, that there was something fundamentally wrong with me. Adults spoke above me about my intrinsic wrongness, my inexplicable strangeness, or in the self-hatred I apparently came with, that's what I heard. I would have nightmares filled with that wrongness, my body misshapen, my hair poisonous snakes snapping at all who came near. The nightmares were so bad I would vomit in my sleep, forcing my mother to wake me every few hours to prevent me from choking to death on my abnormality.

When I was six, my mother was hospitalized for two weeks, exhausted by her life of dealing with the intrinsic racism of her job, and trying to raise two children on her own. For two weeks, I lived with my white Aunty Glynn and her family, where, released from my confused sense of self, I thrived in the loving bedlam of what I had always imagined were only fictional images of family life. In her house, people vocalized their feelings, were clear about right and wrong, and discipline was for when you clearly broke the rules. When my mother recovered, I sobbed for hours, devastated about leaving my aunt and cousins, confused and ashamed about why I didn't want to go home. What was wrong with me that I didn't want to return to my immediate family? My brother, cousins, and aunt tell me that I was a beloved, spoiled princess of whom nothing was expected, and this behavior just underscored that. I saw myself as something far uglier.

Roses and Thorns

I did not belong in my life, or my body, or my home, and I was sure everyone felt the same way about me. I had no friends at Primary School and did not understand how to make any. I suspect now that if I had been tested I would have been found to be on the autism spectrum, but it was the 1970s so I was just weird.

The other kids at school, recognizing my wrongness, called me Medusa and pulled my plaits, laughing when I cried. On my eleventh birthday they all ganged up and stayed away from the only childhood birthday party I ever had. "She just doesn't want to go. My daughter thinks she's too weird," said one mother to mine on the phone.

It is worthy of note that I was one of only two black children in that school; my skin was purely African, my hair the wrong texture, my breasts came in before everyone else's, and my bum stuck out in ways that drew endless mirth. By the time I was eleven I understood that I was irrevocably black, and worse still, African. Nothing about me would ever be acceptable in a country where even my teachers called me a "wog," the British equivalent of "nigger". My family told me that I was the one with the problem; the one who, in my self-absorption, attributed everything to race, who exaggerated reality to make myself the victim. According to them, drowning in my self-hatred, I was unable to see reality at all. It was something that I would hear over and over throughout my life – the claims of over-sensitivity, the accusation of exaggerating my experiences, of only seeing the bad.

The first time I saw God was a relief.

I remember the moment with the imperfect vision of hindsight, the first time those words flashed through my mind like a neon sign blinking dispassionately: "She'd be happier if you were dead," the words circling like unimpeachable knowledge inspired by the phrase I had carried forever, "I do not belong here".

He came to me one morning, his presence sneaking in through the sunlight that struggled through the dirty window pane to settle disinterestedly on the drops of blood liberated from my too-flat nose.

"She'd be happier if you were dead," He whispered in my ear over and over again above the shouting.

I listened and, like a first Holy Communion, I quietly took the remainder of a bottle of Paracetamol, washing it down with a hated glass of warm milk stained pink by the escapees from my still-bleeding nose.

He followed me all the way to school, drawing my eyes to the beauty around me – the dandelion pushing through a cracked paving stone, the bees buzzing around some honeysuckle – and He listed all the people who would be made happier by the end of my existence, because I did not belong and was never meant to be. At the top of that list sat my mother, who would finally be free, with one less ever-needy, ungrateful mouth to feed. Oh, how my death would end her unending unhappiness. I remember how the honey bees kept me company, ready to wing my soul to its rest, as I stumbled, increasingly close to release and school. Since this was 1983, the school nurse sent a clearly sick, possibly hallucinating, eleven-year-old girl home, on her own, a walk that was at least a mile.

But then even God decided He didn't want me.

By the time I had stumbled halfway home, the Paracetamol purged itself from my body and I puked and stumbled my way back to our hellish flat on the edge of London's largest Council Estate (social housing). Hours later, when my mother struggled home, exhausted from another day of trying to provide for an ungrateful child, she appeared unhappy at my continued existence, for in the place of my corpse hung the lingering smell of vomit like an accusatory cloud.

She never knew what her eleven-year-old daughter had done, nor would she know about the other suicide attempts, the binge eating, the cutting, or the depression that simply stood as examples of my failure to be normal like everyone else. My brother and cousin (who spent his holidays from boarding school with us) remember my selfishness, the special treatment I seemed to get, the ways my mother sung my praises when I wasn't there.

They saw my life as a bed of roses; I saw it as a cascade of thorns.

Each moment I existed seemed to inexorably fill me with poison, seeping into my psyche, infecting my experience of the world, until the poison would begin to seep out of me like a slowly exploding volcano.

Finally, I found a purpose for the thorns, a way to expel the poison.

The "self-harm" became a ritual that served to try to bleed out the weirdness, the self-hatred, the devil inside me. Every Sunday afternoon, from the age of thirteen until I left home for university, I would sit on the bathroom floor with a needle, a blade, two pieces of cotton wool, and some TCP antiseptic. On the best days, I would only need to insert the needle under one of my fingernails. The pain was transformative – le petite morte. But it was the welling of blood, the visual bleeding out of the evil inside me that kept me going for another week.

On the worst weeks, it took five little cuts of the blade: four on my inner thigh and one on my wrist. Then the pain would last far longer, stinging with each step I took, and there was always a thrilling risk that I would cut too deeply and bleed out. But after those five cuts I would feel freed for seven more days; until I wasn't.

Each time He came to me and promised to free me, He turned away at the last minute and I survived.

Eventually I turned away from Him, abandoning my faith that He would ever save me from my life, from myself.

But I was lucky in the end. My brother had the unfortunate luck of being born a black male in a world that still despises them. I was a fairly oblivious black girl who lost herself in books, who discovered the one way she could make her mother almost happy was to do well in school, and the knowledge I learned seemed freed from my world. The novels I read did not feature girls who looked like me, the history I studied was devoid of race, and the only historical traumas I was taught featured whites slaughtering each other but not people like me.

Thus, I was an exceptional student.

I was the kind of geek who arrived at school before the gates even opened, who always did the reading and asked questions, who always tried hard to find the right answers. My mother was constantly proud of my grades, and pleased with the fact that I seemed to enjoy studying. Almost every Sunday, she encouraged us with Scrabble games to build our vocabulary and Monopoly to build our maths skills. Whatever else I felt about myself, my intellect seemed the doorway to some sort of acceptance.

Then I learned that the color of my skin trumped my intelligence.

At my final interview at Burntwood School for Girls, the career counselor asked what I wanted to do when I left secondary school. I happily told her that I planned on attending Richmond College and then Oxford University, where I would study Classics and eventually become a solicitor. She smiled and said, "Perhaps you should aim a little lower. Have you considered secretarial school"?

I was stunned.

I had A's in every single course and would go on to win national awards for my drama performance and creative writing. My best friend went in for her interview after me, and left with a pack of college application forms. She had never gotten more than a B in any course, and indeed was pretty much a C student. But she was white and thus apparently deserving of choosing her own future and aspiring to whatever her imagination could conceive. I was black, so my dreams needed to be tempered by the limits of my race – support work, menial labor, but nothing that I was allowed to choose.

I ignored that counselor, seemingly paid to keep me in my place, and set out on my path.

At the first meeting of the Richmond College Oxbridge study group (students could not simply apply to Oxford or Cambridge Universities without jumping through lots of hoops), I excitedly arrived well prepared, having researched my path to university and the steps I would need to be successful. I was, of course, the only person of color in the room of fifteen students. The woman in charge looked me right in the eye and said, "Are you sure you are in the right place"? I assured her I was. "Well, I'm just not sure you would be comfortable at either of these universities. You would be much happier if you applied to a polytechnic where you could do a practical degree". I was so humiliated that I never went back to that room and it started a slow downward spiral of my studies and psyche that ended with a four-day hospital stay during my final exams due to a period that would not stop and mental and physical exhaustion. Just as she and the career officer hoped, I ended up getting two C's and a D in my A-Levels, and thus was rejected by my top university choices. A good (white) friend achieved two D's and an E in her A-Levels and headed off to Oxford University, a journey that would set her up for life welcoming her into the halls of the upper middle class.

I retook two of my A-Levels the next year and achieved A's in both. Then I headed off to Swansea University in South Wales (as far from London as I could get without ending up in Scotland), where I was one of only five students of color in a population of 12,000.

Overall, my experience at Swansea was positive or at least better than my childhood years, freed from the strains of family life. Yes, I hated myself and my social anxiety meant I drank and did drugs to excess, but no more than the average student trying to find themselves. My musical choices and clothing got darker as I ignored my depression, by that point believing the way I felt to be my normality. A stranger among strangers, I was popular in ways I had never been growing up, inexplicably making friends that have lasted to this day. My friends barely acknowledged my race for I was just like them or no different from them than they were from each other (except when we read *Malcom X* and they felt the need to teach me how to be black). Yes, I was called a "nigger" by Swansea locals as they flew past us in their run-down, shitty cars. But Swansea locals hated all students, for we stood as a reflection of the insurmountable class barrier that kept them poor and uneducated. Even more so than in secondary school, I discovered that intellect was valued over almost anything else at university and my intellectual curiosity grew until the thought of being a lifelong scholar became something of an obsession. I began to talk of the day I would buy a little bookstore filled with old secondhand books to keep me company, that no one would ever buy, so that I could spend my life lost in books, pursuing knowledge simply for curiosity's sake.

After university, I tried to find the perfect career for someone like me: a black woman with a degree in American Studies. As my mother ran the temp department at her job, I worked my way through a range of temporary positions where I learned the truth of employment that my mother (and now brother) had already silently experienced. As a black woman, I had to work harder, be more efficient, and dress more conservatively (including relaxed hair, no braids) in order to be considered as acceptable as everyone else. Each job I took on, I transformed my work environment, doing more than I was asked to do, coming up with ideas to make my environment more efficient, arriving earlier and leaving later than anyone else. But it didn't matter. Wherever I worked, it was my white colleagues who got promoted, who were praised for showing up at all. If I took a sick day or arrived late, in every job I was called to my supervisor or manager's office to be reprimanded.

Once again my race, my outside, trumped every other aspect of me.

Finally, after spending two years convincing students of the benefits of graduate study, I decided to be brave and pursue my real passion. Thus, I returned to Swansea University on a full fellowship to pursue my Ph.D. Of course my blackness came with me, as I accidentally discovered a few weeks into the new semester. Arriving in the little prefab building that served the department, I walked in to hear my advisor engaged in a conversation about me. "She's very motivated," said my advisor.

"Well, we thought it was time to have a black student in the department," replied the other voice. "But you know that black students just don't have the academic aptitude for graduate studies, so I don't really expect her to finish". I made my presence known before I had to hear my advisor's reply.

Again I was mortified.

Luckily for me, there were two very different elements at work here that helped my self-esteem. Firstly, my advisor, Craig Phelan, was amazing. He was supportive, motivating, excited about my scholarship, and pushed me to heights that I never could have reached on my own. More than that, he truly believed that I had something to say and had an important contribution to make to the department and the world of African American Studies. Secondly, I was studying the history of racism and the stereotypes of Black women. This was the most politically militant period of my life. Yes, I had monthly emotional breakdowns that the departmental secretary, Bev, had to soothe me through. Yes, I consistently doubted my ability to produce, but my advisor and co-advisor met with me every single Tuesday evening to discuss my readings and ideas. I had support, and most importantly, it was white support (though ironically my advisor was American and my co-advisor was Canadian).

As a result, I became the fastest Ph.D. in American Studies history, completing my dissertation in just three and a half years. Not only that, I became the first Ph.D. to secure a full-time position outside of my department before graduating.

During the period of my graduate studies, the discrimination was implicit and would have gone unnoticed had I not happened to arrive when I did that day. Perhaps because the words doubting my abilities were diminished by the actions of the rest of the department, I could survive and even thrive.

And then I went to America…

A CASE OF AFFIRMATIVE ACTION

I looked up affirmative action once in Wikipedia, and it said, 'A measure by which white men are discriminated against,' and I got so mad. (Gloria Steinem, 2010)

My first academic job almost completed my psychological destruction. As a black British woman who studied racism and stereotypes, accepting a job in Tennessee, the birth place of the Ku Klux Klan, was probably not the best idea, even in 2002. But a job was a job, and I was naively stunned that I had achieved that mythical status of a full-time professor before I had even officially finished my Ph.D. I had only applied because my graduate advisor made me. In 29 years, I had only seen one teacher of color at any level (an English professor when I studied at SUNY Albany for a year). It simply never occurred to me that Africans were allowed to teach, or that it was something I was allowed to aspire to. Yet somehow, I had succeeded on my own merits and based on my own labor, to become that rarified thing: a college professor. Part of me believed that a new start in a new world would do wonders for me. But a central truth of life is that you take yourself with you wherever you go, and I carried my upbringing and all its attendant emotional and psychological damage with me.

On day one, my first day of work in an entirely new culture, my Interim Chair welcomed me by telling me that I was an Affirmative Action hire, and the only reason I got the job was because they were not allowed to hire a white person.

To my face, on my first day.

At the party thrown by the History Department to "welcome" me, a colleague told a joke that was so racist even I was forced to put my British politeness aside to say something. "Oh stop being so sensitive; it's just a joke". To my knowledge, that was the last departmental event they had. When I finally left, I discovered that they (all eight of them) continued to have holiday dinners, summer parties, and random dinner parties at each other's houses; they just didn't invite me because, I guess, I was too sensitive.

There is something very effective about the textures of oppression, constructed to make you feel like the person with the problem, the person with the intrinsic wrongness. Over the course of five long years, it felt like my colleagues systematically set out to destroy every aspect of my psyche, deconstructing and annihilating me to the point of clinical depression. The little cuts that came with every interaction, the microaggressions intended to shoehorn me back into my proper inferior place, the daily reminders that I was not, nor could ever be, good enough for the white halls of academia, all worked to continue my lifelong journey to oblivion.

I hated myself and wanted to die.

The worst, and thus most effective parts, did not come from the Interim Chair, a man who was clearly a standard stereotyped Southern racist and misogynist, a historian who taught that the Civil War was about states' rights not slavery, and that African Americans had been better off when they knew their place. He was easy to dismiss on a personal, if not professional level. His cuts and microaggressions only underscored what I already firmly believed about myself.

No, it was those whom I believed were my allies both within and without the department that were most successful in achieving my destruction.

Within the department, the most painful cuts came from the only other female and other immigrant in the department, who I foolishly believed was my friend. We socialized together, I had Thanksgiving with her family; my mum even had dinner at her house. Yet for five years she socialized with the rest of the department behind my back, never saying a word about what was going on. It even turned out that she had the rest of the department over to her house on multiple occasions. The most insulting was her statement when confronted, that she did not invite me to her dinner parties because my relationship status as a single woman would unbalance her perfect Martha Stewart table setting – apparently an acceptable reason for exclusion in the overtly patriarchal South.

On the outside, the Diversity and Equal Opportunities officer, a large, motherly black woman, looked me in the eye after reading my well-documented report on the racial and sexual harassment I and my students had experienced at the hands of the department, and essentially told me I was being too sensitive and should stop rocking the boat.

Discrimination is a strange self-fulfilling prophecy. The worse things got, the more I believed they were right; and just like at Richmond College, my scholarship suffered. Despite the fact that I consistently scored 5/5 in every student evaluation category (except "grades fairly," I happily admit I am tough), despite the fact that I turned the minor in Africana Studies into a burgeoning program with a broad curriculum with almost as many minors as History had majors, despite the fact that I ran well-attended programs – lectures, movies, televised debates – I was a failure in the eyes of the department. For my first three years, I scored *Excellent* for service and teaching but *Satisfactory* for scholarship. When my fourth year review came around, I was told that it was unlikely I would get tenure because of my lack of collegiality (since I didn't attend the events I knew nothing about, and no one in the department ever attended the events I hosted) and lack of publishing in approved History journals. To put this into context, the last person to earn tenure had only one book chapter, "In Press". He did no work for the college beyond teaching, served on no committees, attended no extracurricular events, yet he was considered worthy of tenure. I had become a famous minnow in a tiny Chattanoogan pond, consistently asked to comment on events for the local press, asked to give talks at the Hunter Museum of Art and the African American Museum of Art and Culture, hosted events for the local black community, and essentially spent innumerable hours raising the profile of the department and the school.

Yet I was not worthy of tenure.

By the end of that review, where my Chair appeared so smug he could barely keep the smile off his face while he listed my inadequacies as a scholar, he announced happily that I had one more year to become the sort of person deserving of a permanent job at UTC. Of course, my core problem was insurmountable. No matter what I did, I would always be the inferior Affirmative Action hire who was only there because no appropriately qualified white person could take the job.

Over those years, the impact of my treatment was both explicit and implicit. My weight ballooned to 350 pounds. I was on blood pressure medication, anti-depressants, and Tramadol for chronic back pain. I was so depressed that to say that I was suicidal seems like a gross understatement. Each day

I contemplated the pros and cons of staying alive. There was a point on my daily commute that was a well-known deathtrap for those not paying attention. Each time I approached that point, I fantasized about taking my hands off the wheel and letting my car smash into the barrier. The only thing that kept me from doing so was the fear that it wouldn't kill me and I would end up a worse burden to those around me.

But I smiled for my friends and buried my pain and humiliation for my students.

I went to Tennessee already trained to believe in my own inadequacies, hoping, I guess, that I could fake it until I made it. This belief in my own inferiority and my own lack of self-esteem worked effectively to ensure I stagnated as a scholar, becoming someone whose work was so tentative and apologetic it is no surprise I had difficulty developing a research profile.

I was what I allowed them to make me.

Yet within that hell, I somehow managed to feed my dying soul by becoming the best teacher I could be, trying to enlighten and inspire my marginalized students, which in the South meant my non-white, female, non-Christian, and gay students. I was everything Southern society still feared in 2006; a single, educated Black woman, with the ability to inform others about their oppression.

I could bury my own oppression, but seeing my students experiencing the same problems I had grown up with broke my heart. I naively told them to make notes of their problems and report them to the Office of Diversity, to be brave and become actors in their own lives. I hosted events about racism on campus and invited core college members. I held a televised debate on Contemporary Southern Racism to a room filled with over 300 people and left in angry tears at the stories I heard.

It was enough.

After four years I put on my big girl pants and started applying for jobs outside of the South (I had learned my lesson). To my amazement, every job I applied for resulted in at least a telephone interview; I got so many on-campus interviews I had to turn down a couple. My biggest concern as I interviewed was the general attitude of the campus. I went to one interview where the students told me not to take the job because the town was so racist they were afraid to cross the train tracks after dark. At another, the students reported that the college specifically discriminated against the students of color in ways that meant they were unlikely to graduate. In short, every campus had its issues with racism but the shades differed depending on a number of factors that helped me make my choice. It was important to me

175

to find a school where I felt as though I could find a support network and make a difference to the marginalized students. Most importantly, I sought a school that recognized its problems and was trying to correct them. After only five minutes with the Chair of Politics and History at Curry College, Larry Hartenian, a European historian and committed Union supporter, I was convinced I had found the right (if not perfect) place.

Perhaps the greatest moment of my life came during my final departmental review with that same Chair (who was no longer Interim). As he began to list all the reasons my hire had been a mistake and the ways I was a fundamental failure, I interrupted him to announce that I had accepted a position elsewhere. His response is worth repeating here because it was so indicative of my experience. "Oh," he said. "Is it a teaching position"? I replied in the affirmative. "Oh. Well, is it at an accredited school"?

That was essentially his last chance. Something in me finally took flight and I realized that, even though I was giving him what he wanted by quitting, I had no intention of going quietly, my head down in shame at my presumption.

For five years, I had taught my students how to cope with prejudice with grace and politeness, to kill the racist with kindness since they would never believe they were filled with prejudice. I told them to record every incidence of racism and report them to the office that was created for just that reason.

Total Bullshit.

I had followed my own rules and all it had done was lead to ridicule, rolled eyes, and disbelief. But I was well-known in the community and on campus; I had a voice that my department had tried to silence. So, on my way out the door, after weeks of my colleagues ignoring me (no leaving party for me), I used my voice for the first time ever. I stopped turning the other cheek; I didn't go gently into that good night. Instead, I sent a campus-wide email in which I outlined my experiences and those of my minority students in excruciating detail. I provided both anecdotal and proven evidence of racist incidents in the classroom, shared by my students with their permission. I listed all the ways I had been discriminated against and racially harassed. I pulled no punches, but kept the email respectful and as devoid of bitterness as I could.

Chattanooga is a small, close-knit town, and the email quickly ended up in the local newspaper with my picture and a lovely bio of the ways the town had seemingly seen me without my knowledge. The article moved me to tears. I had come to see every southerner out of my circle as a small-minded racist who would rather I was gone; yet beyond my department and a few administrators, I was both loved and respected. Ultimately, the email led to a system-wide taskforce to determine if I was right in my claims of rampant institutionalized racism. They discovered that 100% of the non-white hires made at my school in 2002 had subsequently quit as a result of the harassment they had experienced.

I was the last one to flee.

My department collapsed after I left. With the public recognition of my treatment, they were unable to fill my position, even with a white scholar. With the Africana minor removed from the department and moved to Sociology, they began to hemorrhage students. They argued among themselves, refused to hire or keep two faculty who were too politically minded and wanted to end the racism and misogyny. As the most racist members began to retire (or die), the department remained unable to replace it members.

Karma, it seems, really is a bitch.

THE ROAD TO RECOVERY

A basic attribute…was suffering, an agony usually resulting from the torment of being a social misfit. Locked away from the white world, but too closely linked to the black world…[she]sought an answer to an identity problem. That search, seldom successful, led…to emotional destruction and spiritual atrophy. (Melvin Donalson, 1982)

It took a very long time for me to recover from my experiences at the University of Tennessee at Chattanooga. Indeed, it was almost ridiculous to note how destroyed I was when I arrived at my new job at Curry College in Massachusetts. I was so damaged that after my first departmental review I sobbed hysterically, convinced I was going to be fired. When a friend asked what terrible things they had said, I replied that they had been lovely, and had only nice things to say. But they must have been lying. I was so used to the back-stabbing discrimination of UTC that I had trouble taking anything at face value.

Curry College has proven to be the most appropriate space for me to grow and develop as a human being and as a scholar. One of the first things that stands out in dramatic contrast to life in Chattanooga is the simple fact that at Curry, being an intellectual is not considered to be dangerous and being single is not a defining negative characteristic. This could be because Curry is situated in greater Boston, a major city filled with young urban professionals, unlike Chattanooga, a town predicated on family life. That is not to say that Curry College does not have issues. It is a predominantly white school in a predominately white neighborhood with a predominately white

177

staff and an entirely white administration. Students primarily come from majority white towns and majority white schools, and bring with them their parents' conservative ideas about race, class, and sexuality. Thus, we have our issues with racism, homophobia, and misogyny, but unlike Chattanooga, Curry at least acknowledges these as problems, as reflected in the Diversity Task Force Report (2012) and the subsequent relevant parts of the Strategic Plan, which call for an inclusive community.

In my very first semester, I joined the Creative Writing Group, a group which has helped me develop as a writer and thinker, and has given me the confidence to explore both creative writing and academic writing. Members of that group have become a core part of my support network, primarily because of the strong sense of reciprocal respect. In addition, my support network includes primarily women from different walks of life, different races, ethnicities, and nationalities, all of whom have experienced their own issues growing up in a world that still privileges strong patriarchal white ideals. Through making strong friendships (which I also had in Chattanooga), trying to focus on the things that I do well, and trying to listen to the support I received from my colleagues both within the Politics and History department and within the broader school in spaces such as the Diversity Committee and the Faculty Center, I feel as though I've discovered ways in which to leverage my intersectional identity as a black woman, an immigrant who is the child of immigrants, and a scholar.

Yet it took meeting Patricia Leavy in 2009 to begin rebuilding my confidence. She taught me that I have worth, that I have a voice, that I have something of value to add to the world of scholarship. She beat me over the head with my lack of self-esteem until I realized (well, almost) that it is still better to try than to assume failure. Entirely thanks to her tough and funny love, I slowly began to write, present, and generally put my toes back into the shark-infested pool of academia. I discovered my love of Vampiric Scholarship and found a way to connect that to my studies of race. Now I am a well-known scholar in my field. Colleges invite me to give talks, and Warner Brothers even asked me to be a "talking head" for a special anniversary documentary on the classic film *Interview with a Vampire,* where my comments were featured even more than Anne Rice!

In 2012, my apartment burned to the ground, taking my life with it. Finally, I was freed from my past and from all the noxious things that I had brought from my life in the UK and my time in Chattanooga. I felt like a phoenix rising from the ashes, reborn and renewed. As I rebuilt my life, I discovered that I was surrounded by astonishing people who loved and respected me.

People from all around the country sent me gift vouchers, while people at work cooked me meals and blanketed me in support. I finally learned that I am more than the color of my skin, more than my gender, more than my relationship status. I am a person who people like, or at least respect.

One of the greatest lessons of my life has been and remains to be the slow, steady progress to accept myself – not the appearance of acceptance, but the actuality. Thus, I have always confronted my nature and I've always thought deeply about the world around me, but I'm now willing to accept that much of my perspective was filtered through a lens damaged by poor treatment and even poorer support from the adults who were supposed to take care of me as a child and the colleagues who were supposed to be on my side in my work life. I realized that nurture is a significant piece that contributes to our success or failure. My life lessons have taught me that each of us has individual resources, not just outside resources but internal ones as well that provide us with a safe space in our minds to hide out when needed. Children really do need support. Part of growing up is learning to solve problems and stand on your own two feet, but there must be someone there to catch us when we fall, someone to see us when we try to hide. I do not believe I had that as a child, so I turned to my own resources, as immature and imperfect as they were, to provide the support I needed. As a result, adulthood, especially the last ten years, have been an exercise in learning to see myself as I truly am and learning to like that person. This journey has taught me why so many people behave in ways they assume they are supposed to, and live their lives in ways that seem to be correct or normal rather than being free to do as they choose. In that sense, I believe that I am a successful human, for I am now brave enough to do things for myself, not for an external audience.

I am still a work in progress, but it is upward progress. I no longer debate the pros and cons of ending my life, and I have learned to focus on the good in my world and wall off the bad. I am blessed to be at a school that really doesn't care about my scholarship; as a result, I am writing my third book.

But I don't hate myself anymore, nor do I want to die.

And I almost believe that I belong.

SUGGESTED RESOURCES

The author's narrative is heavily informed by the type of biographical work typical in studies of marginalization. The following sources are examples that inspired the author both while growing up and as a professor teaching African American Studies.

DISCUSSION QUESTIONS

The following questions are intended to help draw out some of the deeper issues from Anyiwo's narrative, providing doorways to discussion.

1. In what ways are race and racism constructed differently in the US and UK?
2. How do you explain and understand the gaps between the author's perceptions of herself as a child and her immediate family's perceptions?
3. In what ways were the author's experiences in school indicative of the way minorities are treated in school today? How do her experiences help explain the gap between educational success among whites and minority groups?
4. How do the author's experiences contrast with your own experiences growing up? Who were the people in your life who helped define how you saw yourself? What impact did these people have on your sense of self and the attributes you need to succeed in life?
5. The author refers to ways she tried to cope as a child, including suicide attempts and self-harm. Why do you think the adults were unaware of her actions? Could such circumstances happen in your world growing up without adult support?
6. What were the author's coping strategies to deal with, or push back against, racism in her work settings?
7. Why did the author believe her colleagues at UTC "systematically set out to destroy every aspect of my psyche"? Do you believe that her experiences were explicit or implicit examples of discrimination?
8. What was different about both the author and Curry College that allowed her to feel as though she was on the road to "recovery?"
9. Why do you think the author was able to succeed despite her belief in the multitude of factors set against her?
10. What do you think higher education and work places could do to prevent or more productively respond to the type of racist climates and actions the author describes?

REFERENCES

Angelou, M. (1970). *I know why the caged bird sings*. New York, NY: Random House.
Antonio, A., Astin, H., & Cress, C. (2000). Community service in higher education: A look at the nation's faculty. *Review of Higher Education, 23*(4), 373–398.
Baldwin, R. G. (1996). Faculty career stages and implications for professional development. In D. Finnegan, D. Webster, & Z. F. Gamson (Eds.), *Faculty and faculty issues in colleges and universities* (2nd ed.). Boston, MA: Pearson Custom Publishing.

Berry, D. C. (Producer), & Duke, B. (Director). (2011). *Dark girls* [Motion picture]. United States: Duke Media and Urban Winter Entertainment.

Coates, T. N. (2015). *Between the world and me*. New York, NY: Random House.

Gardner, C., Troupe, Q., & Rivas, M. E. (2006). *The pursuit of happyness*. New York, NY: Amistad.

McCall, N. (1994). *Makes me wanna holler: A young Black man in America*. New York, NY: Random House.

Morison, S. E. (1936). *Harvard College in the seventeenth century*. Cambridge, MA: Harvard University Press.

Morrison, T. (1994). *The bluest eye*. New York, NY: Plume Book.

Upshal, D. (Producer). (1998). *Windrush* (Pt. 1). London: BBC.

Valerius, D., Morales, M., & Femme, N. (Production). (2008). *The souls of Black girls* [Motion picture]. United States: Femme Noire Production.

Wilson, H. E. (1990). *Our nig: Or, sketches from the life of a free black, in a two-story white house, north: Showing that slavery's shadows fall even there*. Champaign, IL: Project Gutenberg.

ABOUT THE CONTRIBUTORS

EDITOR

Patricia Leavy, Ph.D., is an independent scholar (formerly Associate Professor of Sociology, Chair of Sociology & Criminology, and Founding Director of Gender Studies at Stonehill College). She is an internationally recognized leader in the fields of arts-based research and research methodology. She is the author or editor of more than twenty books, including *Research Design: Quantitative, Qualitative, Mixed Methods, Arts-Based, and Community-Based Participatory Approaches* (Guilford Press, 2017), *Method Meets Art: Arts-Based Research Practice, Second Edition* (Guilford Press, 2015), *The Oxford Handbook of Qualitative Research* (Oxford University Press, 2014), and the novels *Low-Fat Love* (Sense Publishers 2011; 2015), *American Circumstance* (Sense Publishers, 2013, 2016), and *Blue* (Sense Publishers, 2016). She has earned critical and commercial success in both nonfiction and fiction, and her books have been translated into many languages. She is also series creator and editor for seven book series with Oxford University Press and Sense Publishers, including the groundbreaking *Social Fictions* series. Known for her commitment to public scholarship, she is frequently called on by the U.S. national news media and writes regular blogs for *The Huffington Post, The Creativity Post*, and *We Are the Real Deal*. She has received career awards from the New England Sociological Association, the American Creativity Association, the American Educational Research Association, and the International Congress of Qualitative Inquiry. In 2016, Mogul, a global women's empowerment network, named her an "Influencer." Her website is: www.patricialeavy.com.

CONTRIBUTORS

Tony E. Adams is Professor, Department of Communication at Bradley University. He studies and teaches about interpersonal and family communication, autoethnography, qualitative research, communication theory, and sex, gender, and sexuality. He is the author of *Narrating the Closet: An Autoethnography of Same Sex Desire* (Routledge, 2011) and co-author, with Stacy Holman Jones and Carolyn Ellis, of *Autoethnography* (Oxford University Press, 2014). He also co-edited, with Stacy Holman Jones and Carolyn Ellis, *Handbook of Autoethnography* (Routledge, 2013) and co-edited, with Jonathan Wyatt, *On (Writing) Families: Autoethnographies of Presence and Absence, Love and Loss* (Sense Publishers, 2014).

U. Melissa Anyiwo is Professor of Politics & History and Coordinator of African American Studies at Curry College in Massachusetts. A transplanted Nigerian-British citizen with a background in race, gender, diversity, and visual archetypes, she regularly writes and presents on vampires and their connection to gender stereotypes, including *Bad Girls? Selene and the Redeeming of the Female Vampire in the Underworld Series*. Her published work on vampires includes the chapter, "It's Not Television, it's Transmedia Storytelling: Marketing the 'Real' World of True Blood" in *True Blood: Investigating Vampires and the Southern Gothic* (I.B. Tauris, 2012). She has also published the edited collections *Buffy Conquers the Academy* (Cambridge Scholars Press, 2013), *Race in the Vampire Narrative* (Sense, 2015), and *Gender in the Vampire Narrative* (Sense, 2016). Finally, she starred in the documentary *Lestat, Louis, and the Vampire Phenomenon* for the Interview with the Vampire 20th Anniversary Edition DVD (Warner Brothers, 2014).

Lisa Barry, Ph.D., is a lecturer in Communication at California State University Channel Islands. She has twenty years' teaching experience, and her scholarship focuses on images of women and minorities in American media, as well as the rhetoric of Eleanor Roosevelt.

Tammy Bird lives in Wendell, North Carolina with her wife and two cats. She is an educator by day and a writer by night. She has a deep passion for working with students, which includes helping them to understand and describe life through storytelling in an attempt to spread through words the beauty of inclusivity. In addition to contributing to educational anthologies, she has published several short stories and hopes to soon publish her first novel.

Kate Birdsall was born in the heart of the Rust Belt and harbors a hesitant affinity for its grit. She's an existentialist who writes both short and long fiction and creative nonfiction, and she plays a variety of loud instruments. She lives in Michigan's capital city with her partner and at least one too many four-legged creatures. She teaches writing of all kinds (first-year, professional, and creative) at Michigan State University.

Robin M. Boylorn, Ph.D. is Associate Professor of Interpersonal and Intercultural Communication at the University of Alabama. Her research and teaching focuses on issues of social identity and diversity, focusing primarily on the lived experience of black women. Her work has appeared in *Qualitative Inquiry*, *Cultural Studies ↔ Critical Methodologies*, *Critical Studies in Media Communication*, *International Review of Qualitative Research*, and *Departures in Critical Qualitative Research*. She is the author of *Sweetwater: Black Women and Narratives of Resilience* and co-editor of *Critical Autoethnography: Intersecting Cultural Identities in Everyday Life*.

Venus E. Evans-Winters, Ph.D., is Associate Professor of Education at Illinois State University in the Department of Educational Administration and Foundations. Dr. Evans-Winters is also faculty affiliate with the departments of Women & Gender

Studies and Ethnic Studies. Her research interests are school resilience, urban education policy and practice, and the schooling of Black girls and women. Dr. Evans-Winters teaches in the areas of education policy studies, qualitative research, and social foundations of education. She is the author of *Teaching Black Girls: Resilience in Urban Classrooms*, and co-editor of the books *(Re)Teaching Trayvon: Education for Social Justice & Human Freedom* and *Black Feminism in Education: Black Women Speak Back, Up, and Out*. She was invited to the White House to participate in a meeting with the White House Council on Women and Girls, and is the author of numerous academic articles and book chapters.

Donna Y. Ford, Ph.D., is Professor and Endowed Chair of Education and Human Development at Vanderbilt University. Dr. Ford currently holds a joint appointment in the Department of Special Education and Department of Teaching and Learning. She earned her Doctor of Philosophy degree in Urban Education (educational psychology) in 1991, Masters of Education degree (counseling) in 1988, and Bachelor of Arts degree in communications and Spanish in 1984 from Cleveland State University. Dr. Ford conducts research primarily in gifted education and multicultural/urban education. Specifically, her work focuses on the achievement gap, recruiting and retaining culturally different students in gifted education, multicultural curriculum and instruction, culturally competent teacher training and development, Black identity, and Black family involvement. She consults with school districts and educational and legal organizations on such topics as under-representation in gifted education and Advanced Placement, multicultural/urban education and counseling, and closing the achievement gap. She is the author/co-author of several books and numerous articles and chapters.

Sarrah J. Grubb has spent the last 16 years working in PK-12 education in private and public schools in three different states. Since 2004, she has devoted her work to public schools in rural areas and students at risk due to poverty. As a K-12 Gifted Specialist, and later a K-12 Curriculum, Instruction, and Professional Development Coordinator, she worked to show the strengths of rural populations and help teachers instruct for success with their students. In 2016 she received her Ph.D from Miami University in Oxford, OH, and teaches preservice teacher candidates in her appointment as Assistant Professors of Education at Alice Lloyd College.

Jean Kilbourne is internationally recognized for her groundbreaking work on the image of women in advertising and for her critical studies of alcohol and tobacco advertising. In the late 1960s, she began her exploration of the connection between advertising and several public health issues, including violence against women, eating disorders, and addiction, and launched a movement to promote media literacy as a way to prevent these problems. A radical and original idea at the time, this approach is now mainstream and an integral part of most prevention programs. She is the creator of the renowned *Killing Us Softly: Advertising's Image of Women* film series (and several other films), and is the author of the award-winning book *Can't Buy My Love: How Advertising Changes the Way We Think and Feel* and *So Sexy So Soon: The New Sexualized Childhood and What Parents Can Do to Protect Their Kids*. She holds an honorary position as Senior Scholar at the Wellesley Centers for Women. In 2015 she was inducted into the National Women's Hall of Fame.

Nancy La Monica recently earned a Ph.D. in Human Geography. Her educational background in Sociology (B.A.) and Critical Disability Studies (M.A.) combined with her passion for social inclusion and social justice enable Nancy to advocate on behalf of disabled students who face social, institutional, and economic barriers to access of higher education. In her doctoral research, she used autoethnography, combined with qualitative data collected through online methods, to explore the experience of navigating the emotional geographic space of graduate school for non-visibly disabled students, including those with learning disabilities and mental health disabilities at two southern Ontario universities. An integral part of her work includes exploring the emotion work and emotional labor that students do as they contend with processes of disablement in academia. Moving forward, she hopes to continue this work to include non-visibly disabled faculty members. Currently, she teaches at Seneca College in Toronto.

Mayme Lefurgey is a Ph.D. candidate at Western University in London, Ontario, Canada. She is pursuing a collaborative degree in Women's Studies & Feminist Research and Transitional Justice & Post-Conflict Reconstruction. She holds a B.A. in Sociology from Mount Allison University in Canada, an M.A. in Gender and Peacebuilding from the University for Peace in Costa Rica, and an M.A. in International Conflict Transformation from the University of Innsbruck in Austria. Mayme's work and volunteer experiences have taken her to Costa Rica, Honduras, Nepal, Tanzania, and Malawi, where she has been involved with various campaigns and projects in the field of international women's rights. She has worked extensively with the UK-based African-diaspora organization, Make Every Woman Count. She currently works with the international organization Omprakash, mentoring undergraduate students seeking to volunteer abroad, via an online critical education platform. Mayme's academic interests include global women's rights, organizing and collaboration, critical peace and development studies, and feminist pedagogy.

Shalen Lowell is a transgender writer, blogger, and poet hailing from Boston, Massachusetts, and specializes in queer literature and fiction that represents the intersection of fantasy and postmodern genres. Shalen earned their B.A. in English Literature from Stonehill College, and their work also focuses on the crises of environmental degradation as figured through fantasy media. In addition to working full-time as a marketing copy writer and project assistant for author/editor Dr. Patricia Leavy, Shalen has published numerous short stories in their post-graduate career, most notably publishing with *Aether and Ichor* and *The Writing Disorder*.

miroslav pavle manovski, Ph.D., is an author, baritone, K-12 public school music educator, teacher of voice, and independent scholar of arts-based, autoethnographic and qualitative research. He was also the 2012-2015 co-chair of Gender Research in Music Education international (GRIME) and the recipient of the 2013 Outstanding Dissertation Award from the Arts-Based Educational Research (ABER) Special Interest Group of the American Educational Research Association (AERA). Dr. manovski earned his Bachelor of Music and Master of Music in Performance (Voice) at the University of Michigan in Ann Arbor and his Philosophy Doctorate in Music Education at Oakland University in Rochester, MI. He is currently the general and vocal music teacher with Birmingham Public Schools, MI and sings professionally with the chorus of the Michigan Opera Theatre at the Detroit Opera House. To learn more, please visit www.miroslav.me or contact him directly via email: miroslav.pavle.manovski@gmail.com.

Amy L. Masko, Ph.D., is a professor at Grand Valley State University in Allendale, Michigan. She earned her Ph.D. from the University of Denver in Curriculum and Instruction with an emphasis in Urban Education, and her M.Ed. from Lesley University in Curriculum and Instruction with an emphasis in Literacy Education. Her research interests include the intersection of race, poverty, and schooling, Critical Race Theory, and comparative international education. She has written articles about urban and rural education in both the United States and Ghana, West Africa. She has worked for public schools and community-based educational non-profits. She currently teaches courses in English education at Grand Valley.

Lisa A. Phillips is a psychologist specializing in children and family services in Pennsylvania. She is the clinical director of a large community mental health center where she oversees the training of doctoral interns, psychology residents, and all outpatient treatment programs.

Christopher N. Poulos, Ph.D., is Professor and Head of the Department of Communication Studies at the University of North Carolina at Greensboro. An ethnographer and philosopher of communication, he teaches courses in relational and family communication, ethnography, dialogue, and film. His award-winning book, *Accidental Ethnography: An Inquiry into Family Secrecy*, was published by Left Coast Press in 2009. His work has appeared in *Qualitative Inquiry, Communication Theory, Southern Communication Journal, International Review of Qualitative Research, Qualitative Communication Research*, and in several edited books.

Em Rademaker currently works as the Residence Life Coordinator for the University of Alaska Southeast. They hold a Bachelor of Arts in German and Classical

Civilization and will complete a Master of Public Administration degree. Em intends to pursue a career in public policy development and implementation, specifically as it relates to underrepresented groups. Em is passionate about LGBTQ+ education and advocacy and has incorporated this work into their current and previous positions, developing Safe Zone programs and Gender Inclusive Housing policies. In their personal life, Em enjoys music, travel, and exploring the great wilderness of Alaska with their dog, Ranma.

Liza A. Talusan, Ph.D., is a Boston-based writer, teacher, and facilitator. She has twenty years of experience working in PK-12 and higher education environments, guiding conversations and action-oriented steps towards creating a more just, equitable, and inclusive community. Through identity-conscious practices, Dr. Talusan focuses on exploring how individuals connect to issues of diversity, equity, and inclusion by creating personal connections to institutional issues. She earned her B.A. from Connecticut College, M.A. from New York University, and Ph.D. from University of Massachusetts Boston. Liza was featured in the documentary film *I'm Not Racist ... Am I?*

Adrienne Trier-Bieniek, Ph.D., is Chair of Sociology and Anthropology at Valencia College. She is the author of *Sing Us a Song, Piano Woman: Female Fans and the Music of Tori Amos* (Scarecrow 2014), and has edited several books focused on gender and culture including *The Beyoncé Effect* (McFarland 2016) and *Feminist Theory and Pop Culture* (Sense 2015). Her research has appeared in *Qualitative Research* and she regularly contributes to public scholarship by writing for websites, including *The Huffington Post* and *The Mary Sue*. www.adriennetrier-bieniek.com